AF541753

ORGANISATIONAL CLIMATE

ORGANISATIONAL CLIMATE

By

Dr. M. Edwin Gnanadhas

M.Com, M.Phil, Ph.D.
Deptt. of Commerce
Scott Christian College
Nagercoil
Tamil Nadu

&

Dr. A. Arockia Dass

Associate Professor
Deptt. of Commerce
St. Xavier's College, Palayamkottai
Tamil Nadu

DISCOVERY PUBLISHING HOUSE PVT. LTD.
NEW DELHI-110 002

Published by:
Tilak Wasan

DISCOVERY PUBLISHING HOUSE PVT. LTD.
4831/24, Prahlad Street, Ansari Road
Darya Ganj, New Delhi-110002 (India)
Phone : +91-11-23279245, 43764432
Fax : +91-11-23253475
E-mail : parul.wasan@gmail.com
discoverypublishinghouse@gmail.com
info@discoverypublishinggroup.com
web : www.discoverypublishinggroup.com

First Edition: **2011**
ISBN: 978-81-8356-885-2

Organisational Climate

Printed at:
Shree Balaji Art Press
Delhi

Preface

Lewin *et al.* (1939) introduced the concept of 'climate' into the vocabulary of social psychology and it was used to describe the attitudes, feelings and social processes that occurred among groups of boys at an American summer camp. They used the term social climate and social atmosphere interchangeably to connote the psychological conditions created by leaders of boys' group. Organisational climate is a set of properties of the work environment perceived directly or indirectly by the employee that is assumed to be a major force in influencing employee behaviour. It is the recurring patterns of behaviour, attitudes and feelings that characterise life in the organisation. The concept of organisational climate is currently being used to describe configuration of attitudes and perceptions by organisation members that, in combination, reflect a substantial part of the context of which they are a part and within which they work. A study of organisational climate identifies the variables which moderate an organisations' ability to mobilise its work force inorder to achieve business goals and maximise performance.

A good climate is a prerequisite for the organisational success which is marketing either a product or service. It is all the more important in rendering service and the service provider should think beyond mere fulfilment of expectations of those who come into contact with an organisation. In organisations such as transportation, both the employees and the commuters experience a climate, employees with regard to the emphasis on service excellence they experience and commuters with regard to the experience they have when served, including the level of service quality they receive.

An attempt has been made in this book to identify the over all look out of employees towards the various dimensions of organisational climate prevailing in a transport undertaking. It is believed that such an attempt would help transport undertakings to take stock of the situation with a view to improve the climate and thereby reach greater heights in the process of rendering better service to commuters.

We gratefully thank Dr. S. Chellakumar Rose, Principal, Scott Christian College (Autonomous), Nagercoil who has been a source of inspiration for all our academic activities. We thank all our friends and well-wishers who have encouraged and helped us in one way or other for this publication.

We also express our sincere thanks to Dr. X. Antony Thanaraj, Associate Professor, Department of Commerce, Scott Christian College, Nagercoil, Tamil Nadu for his valuable guidance and encouragement.

We also take this opportunity to thank Shri Tilak Wasan, Director, Discovery Publishing House Pvt. Ltd, New Delhi for his initiatives in bringing out this book.

M. EDWIN GNANADHAS
A. AROCKIA DASS

Contents

Introduction and Design of the Study

Introduction

The term 'climate' in a natural sense refers to the condition of the weather at a place over a period of years, which is exhibited by temperature, velocity of wind and precipitation. Organisational climate is a set of measurable properties of the work environment perceived directly or indirectly by the people who live and work in the environment and assumed to influence their motivation and behaviour. Organisational climate within an organisation refers to how organisational environments are perceived and interpreted by its employees.

The concept 'organisational climate' is also explained as the perceptions that employees share about what is important in an organisation obtained through their experiences on the job and their perceptions of the kind of behaviour the management expects and supports. Organisational climate consists of a set of characteristics that describes an organisation and distinguishes it from other organisations. A set of attributes to a particular organisation may be induced from the behaviour and attitude in which the organisation deals with its members. Individual perception of organisational properties and organisational factors is the major determinant of climate in an organisation.

It was Tagiuri (1968) who provided a research based definition of 'organisational climate'. According to him 'organisational climate is a relatively enduring quality of the internal environment of an organisation that (*a*) is experienced by its members, (*b*) influences their behaviour and (*c*) can be described in terms of the values of a particular set of characteristics of the organisation.'

Moran and Volkwein (1992) defined organisational climate as 'relatively enduring characteristics of an organisation which distinguish it from other organisations and (*a*) embody members' collective perceptions about their organisation with respect to such dimensions as autonomy, trust, cohesiveness, support, recognition, innovation and fairness; (*b*) are produced by member interaction; (*c*) serve as a basis for interpreting the situation; (*d*) reflect the prevalent norms and attitudes of the organisation's culture; and (*e*) act as a source of influence for shaping behaviour.'

Organisational climate as suggested by West *et al.* (1998) refers to the 'Perceptions that organisation members share of fundamental elements of their organisation'.

Origin of Work Climate

Truly great ideas stand the test of time becoming seasoned and more effective as they are shared, passed on and built upon by others. This certainly holds true for the concept of 'work climate' with its rich history and impressive circle of researchers, educators and practitioners. The idea of work climate arises from social psychology, a field of psychology that studies the nature and causes of human behaviour as it relates to people in groups and society as a whole. Unlike sociology, whose focus is groups, social psychology also looks at the individual in groups.

The first mention of psychological climate occurred when Kurt Lewin, one of the founding fathers of social psychology, used the phrase 'social atmosphere' in studying the effectiveness of work groups. It was Lewin who first established the 'empirical reality' of the social atmosphere within a group and its powerful impact on how members of a group interact. Lewin was also one of the first to establish that social atmosphere (what was to become the term 'climate') was an essential, functional link between the person and their work environment.

Later during the 1950s and 60s researchers such as Robert Stringer, George Litwin, Renato Tagiuri, David McClelland and John Atkinson deepened our insights into how work climate impacts work experiences and also linked its dynamics to human motivation. This further research proved that energised motivation drives superior performance and ultimately impacts financial business outcomes. A leader, or even an organisation, wants more of a desired behaviour from a group or an individual, such as demonstrating a drive for high personal standards.

The work of Tagiuri, Litwin, Stringer, McClelland, Atkinson and others eventually provided measurable linkage between organisational climate, motivation, performance and financial outcomes. Research proved that motivation resides within people and that part of their environment, called Work Climate, arouses and energizes this motivation. Once the concept of Organisational Work Climate was linked to measurable financial outputs, Corporate America took serious notice.

Work Climate Drives Motivation

During the 1950s and 60s, psychologists David McClelland (first at Wesleyan University and later at Harvard) and John Atkinson (at the University of Michigan) focused on research that established the relationship between work climate and its impact on human motivation, with particular emphasis on what they identified as the Acheivement Motivation.

Tagiuri's research also found that climate exists within every organisation as part of the organisation and is perceived in a subjective manner by the people in the organisation. He acknowledged climate as an 'experience' - it is a perception.

And since it is a subjective experience, climate can only be known indirectly through the collective perception of the members of the organisation. Tagiuri directed his attention towards a pragmatic realisation that these perceptions, though subjective, can be measured and managed and referred these subjective perceptions as 'climate'.

A Simple Formula

Robert Stringer and George Litwin took Tagiuri's work a step further. Through their rigorous research at Harvard Business School, they declared that work climate is not only a powerful influence of behaviour in an organisation, but a determinant of human motivation. This was a major breakthrough in the history of work climate and gave rise to the following formula:

$$B = M \times E$$

The (B)ehaviour (performance) people demonstrate is equal to the (M)otivational Drivers (power, achievement, affiliation) they carry within themselves, influenced by the (E)nvironment (climate) in which they work.

The ongoing research shows the critical linkage between organisational work climate and the creation of a perceptual platform to arouse, drive and direct the motivation to achieve. Doing things better, outperforming others, deciding on internal standards of excellence and realistic goal accomplishment are the behaviours that today's organisations require in order to meet the demands of a whole new competitive global market. The research of Taugiri, Litwin, Stringer, McClellannd, Atkinson and others have provided a new paradigm of human motivation and performance at work.

A new simple model was introduced that delineated :

Climate = Motivation = Behaviour = Outcome

Motivation was no longer viewed as something extrinsic. The idea that a leader could motivate his employees lost its significance and the carrot-and-stick model became outdated. Instead, research showed that motivation resides within people at all times. For groups at work, there exists a unique part of their overall environment, called work climate, that arouses and energises this motivation into action and thereby laying the foundation for superior performance. Motivation is now an 'arousal' model over which managers, leaders and individuals could have direct influence. The field of motivational study would never be the same.

Work climate plays a vital role in deciding the effectiveness in performance. Today, practitioners and researchers continue to discover new ways in which work climate influences such diverse areas as innovation, stress reduction, trust, strategic thinking, team cohesion, turnover reduction, conflict mediation, call center effectiveness, goal attainment and educational systems etc.

In 2001, the Hay Group of Boston, Massachusetts, conducted an updated and extensive study on the impact of organisational climate in high performing organisations. Their results showed that up to 70 per cent of the perception of organisational climate comes from the quality of leadership extended by the organisations. The research also highlighted that work climate can be directly linked to contributing upto 30 per cent of the organisation's financial revenue. Other studies have supported this approximate 30 per cent impact upon business outputs.

Robert Stringer, one of the original researchers into work climate at Harvard, remains a devotee to his earlier work and continues till today to consult and write on the subject. In his newest book *Leadership and Organisational Climate*, Stringer uses the following brief and simple definition of modern work climate: 'Organisational climate is the collection and pattern of the environmental determinants of aroused motivation'.

The definitions and theoretical positions on climate have varied considerably between individual theorists. This has also been the case for the dimensions of climate and its measurement. Developing a universal set of dimensions applicable to all situations was the central issue of the climate researchers so as to enable comparative studies in different organisational settings. Jones and James (1979) have identified conflict and ambiguity, job challenge, importance and variety, leader facilitation and support, workgroup co-operation, friendliness and warmth, professional and organisational esprit and job standards as dimensions of organisational climate.

Ryder and Southey (1990) have identified leader facilitation and support, job variety, challenge and esprit, conflict and pressure, organisational planning and openness, workgroup reputation, co-operation, friendliness and warmth and perceived equality as the dimensions of organisational climate. Though researchers and academicians have identified the role of organisational climate in the performance of an organisation, there is no unanimous opinion among them regarding uniformity of dimensions affecting organisational climate irrespective of the nature of the organisation.

Organisational climate has its major influence on the performance of the workforce which is determined by the level of its satisfaction and motivation. It can be used as a management tool to provide managers with many insights into how their employees regard their organisation. Creation of a positive work atmosphere in an organisation is a long term proposition and administrators should take an asset approach in this direction.

Creation of a favourable work atmosphere by the management is possible only if it understands the changing scenario, growing awareness among employees on different issues concerning employment, intensity of competition among the producers and marketers due to preference for quality in products and services offered, possible impact on effecting continuous changes in the composition of workforce and the increased avenues which are open to the workforce to move towards the destinations where handsome packages are offered to attract the best talents and retain them for a reasonable period if not for their life time.

There are four mechanisms by which organisational climate affects the performance, satisfaction and attitudes of people in an organisation. They are:

1. Organisational variables can act as a constrained system and provide knowledge to the participants regarding certain types of behaviour which will be rewarded, punished or ignored. Different rewards and punishments may be given for different kinds of behaviour and it is only through this kind of response that an organisation can influence the behaviour of its participants.
2. Organisational variables may guide a person to conduct an evaluation of self and others to make him realise the actual state of his achievement and this will definitely influence his behaviour.
3. Organisational factors work as stimuli which can influence the individual's arousal level, activation and performance.
4. Organisational variables can influence the individuals to form a perception of the organisation and such a condition can further influence the behaviour of the employees.

A sound climate is a long-term proposition. It is the organisational behaviour system which acts as a corner stone for building a climate in an organisation. The concept of organisation behaviour derives its strength from both fact and value premises. Fact premises represent how human beings behave, while value premises represent the desirability of certain goals. Organisational climate exists in a contingency relationship where it depends upon the type of people it has, the kind of technology it uses, the level of education it imparts and the expectation of the collaborators. In dealing with people, the total man concept should be borne in mind which is a combination of three different concepts about the nature of human beings viz., economic, social and self-fulfilling. In order to build up a conducive organisational climate, the managers must understand their human force in a better way and efforts should be taken to identify what motivates their job performance. Having a keen insight into the minds of individuals, designing a personal approach in leadership and job design are the other aspects of consideration in the process of building a favourable climate in an organisation.

Statement of the Problem

Watkin and Habbard (2003) after nearly 35 years of consulting field research observe that organisational climate and performance are linked and that climate can directly account for up to 30 per cent of the variance in key business performance measures. Work climate now a days is more important than it was previously because the external and internal environments of work organisations are less stable and less predictable than before. Hence, the major challenges of today's managers are to get things done in such a hostile, continuously changing work environments and to create a climate in which employees volunteer their creativity and expertise. Because of the increasing competition for high performing workers and the changing life styles of the workforce, most companies are amending their policies to better accommodate the demands of the workforce.

Providing a conducive work atmosphere coupled with an attractive salary package enables the workforce to feel pleasant about their work and this could lead to improved individual efficiency and overall organisational performance. Some organisations even use climate as a proxy measure when performance is difficult to quantify. In such cases, climate assessment provides an invaluable profit and loss statement on how well a company manages its people. Organisations across the world, therefore are on the lookout for methods and measures which could enhance the quality of organisational climate. Any initiative on the part of an organisation to diagnose what is actually present in the form of opinions, observations etc., of its workforce on anything concerning their work will disclose its strength and weakness.

Diagnosis of the strength and weakness would enable an organisation to identify where it gets deviated from the actual expectations of the workforce and to measure the effect of such deviations which are generally brought out in the form of reduced interest in work, failing to raise oneself upto the performance level expected, influencing negatively the fellow workers to turn against the work and organisation and finally leaving the organisation prematurely etc. Popular initiatives such as Total Quality Management (TQM) and Six Sigma are opted for and implemented by organisations to induce favourable changes in the environment of the organisations because of the human interventions involved in their implementation process. Burruss (1996) argues that managing for motivation and performance improvement is essential for work organisations, and that improving a supportive work climate is directly related to employee's motivation and performance. He further argues that when the environment is positive, people are motivated and excited about what they are doing. However when it is negative, people are relatively depressed and angry. Therefore it is clear that work climate is an excellent predicator of an organisation as well as employee performance.

Objectives

The following are the main objectives of the study :

(*i*) To find out the perception of employees towards the various dimensions of organisational climate.

(*ii*) To study the relationship between the perception and socio-economic factors of employees.

(*iii*) To identify the influence of organisational climate on motivation and performance of employees.

(*iv*) To examine the relationship between the perception and the understanding of the basic job requisites possessed by the employees.

(*v*) To know the preference of employees over the different aspects of work life which have an impact on organisational climate.

Hypotheses

The following are the hypotheses formulated for the study:

1. There is no significant difference in the perception of employees towards the various dimensions of organisational climate on the basis of socio-economic factors.
2. There is no significant difference in ranking the different aspects of work life by employees on the basis of socio-economic factors.

Methodology

This section describes the methodology adopted in the present study which includes the choice of study area, sampling technique adopted, collection of data, period of study and tools used for analysis.

Choice of Study Area

The work climate in an organisation is a vital element which influences the perception and behaviour of its work force either favourably or unfavourably and transport service organisations are not an exception in this regard. Since transport, especially passenger transport, comes under the service sector, it has a major role to play in the nation building exercise by ensuring safe, smooth and uninterrupted service to the public. The transport sector services in Tamil Nadu are shared by private operators and government undertakings and the transport service in metropolitan city of the state is vested fully in the hands of government undertakings.

The competition among the private bus operators is intense due to improved collection and the role of drivers and conductors in this regard is significant. Dedication, punctuality, good rapport with commuters, flexibility, spirit of competition and untiring service are some of the good qualities on the part of the private bus operators which ultimately have made them excel government undertakings involved in bus operation.

Though all the government transport undertakings in Tamil Nadu have a band of skilled work force, a few of them are running at loss today. It has been identified that they earn a decent income by their bus operations but they still face financial crunch due to some reasons. One among the reasons is the poor internal support they receive from their employees.

The character of an organisation's work environment (particularly as perceived by its members) has long been recognised as a potent influence on employee cognition, attitude and behaviours. It has been learnt that a large number of characteristics of positive organisational work environment which influence the members' cognition, attitudes and behaviours are missing in Government owned transport undertakings, more particularly in Tamil Nadu State Transport Corporation located in Tirunelveli District. The work climate in this region is rigid, uncordial, mutually not supportive, not trustworthy, heading towards hostility and any delay in recognising these unfavourable developments and implementing appropriate corrective measures would lead the Corporation to face a disaster which cannot be set right in a short span of time.

Sampling Technique

The choice of an appropriate sampling technique is vital in any research endeavour and keeping this in mind, the researcher has adopted the stratified simple random sampling method with proportionate allocation for the present study. The Tamil Nadu State Transport Corporation, Tirunelveli District has eight depots in different parts of the district viz., Thenkasi, Pulliangudi, Sankarankovil, Papanasam, Valliyoor.

K.T.C. Nagar, By-pass Road and Thamiraparani. The total strength of the employees was 3091 in the year 2007. The employees of the Corporation are engaged in three major kinds of work namely operation of buses, maintenance of buses and office administration. Among them, the strength of employees engaged in bus operation is higher than the strength of employees engaged in bus maintenance. The total number of employees engaged in administrative work is limited when compared to the number of employees involved in bus operation and bus maintenance. This unequal size of the population in the three major categories of work has urged the researcher to give proportionate representation in the selection of the sample and thus 300 employees were selected for the present study.

Collection of Data

The data required for the present study was collected through primary and secondary sources. The primary data was collected from respondents through a well structured questionnaire which was pre-tested before it was employed in the field for data collection. The questionnaire was designed after reviewing the related literature and previous studies conducted in the subject area by different researchers. The questionnaire includes various aspects like socio-economic factors, dimensions of organisational climate, role of the prevailing organisational climate in motivation and performance of employees, perception towards the basic job requisites possessed by employees and the preference of employees over the different aspects of work life which have an impact on organisational climate.

All the questions posed to the respondents were designed as positive statements. Likert's five point scaling technique consisting of responses from 'Strong Agreement' to 'Strong

Disagreement' has been used to gauge the perception of employees towards organisational climate.

A strong conceptual understanding, deciding the content to be studied relevant to the research problem under consideration, and the particular direction to be taken in search of solutions for the problem highly depend on the understanding developed by the researcher in his area of study. Secondary data are essential for such an understanding. As far as the present study is concerned, the researcher has collected the secondary data from text books, research papers published in journals, policy notes issued by the Tamil Nadu State Transport Corporation on behalf of the Government of Tamil Nadu, pamphlets and booklets.

Period of Study

The present study entitled *Organisational Climate* was conducted between the years 2007 and 2008.

Tools of Analysis

The selection and application of appropriate statistical tools ensure reliability of data collected and appropriateness of solutions suggested to the problem under consideration. In order to ensure internal consistency and reliability of items in a scale, Cronbach's Alpha test of reliability was applied by the researcher. Kruskal Wallis test was applied to find out the difference in the perception of employees towards various dimensions of organisational climate on the basis of socio-economic factors. Arithmetic mean, standard deviation, co-efficient of variation, chi-square, correlation and t-test are the other statistical techniques used in the study for data analysis.

Limitations of the Study

1. The availability of data and the co-operation of respondents are important for the success of any research endeavour aiming at offering appropriate

suggestions for the problem under consideration. In the present study, it was observed that the co-operation of a section of respondents either for filling in the questionnaire or for personal interaction was limited. The initiative of the researcher to gather additional information from the trade unions would have been a great success if all the trade unions had participated in the deliberations.

2. The Tamil Nadu State Transport Corporation, Tirunelveli division has Tirunelveli and Tuticorin districts as its operational area. The present study was conducted in Tirunelveli district and Tuticorin district was kept out of the purview of the study.
3. The present study takes into account only the perception of employees towards the various aspects responsible for deciding the quality of work climate prevailing in Tamil Nadu State Transport Corporation, Tirunelveli district.

Chapterisation

The report of the study entitled 'Organisational Climate' is presented in seven chapters.

The first chapter 'Introduction and design of the study' introduces the concept and deals with the various areas of the design of the study viz., statement of problem, objectives, hypotheses, methodology, limitations and chapterisation.

The second chapter 'Review of related literature' presents the collection of advanced literature related to the study including a review of the previous studies conducted by other researchers in the subject area.

The third chapter 'Profile of the study unit' gives an account of information related to Tamil Nadu State Transport Corporation, Tirunelveli district.

The fourth chapter 'Perceptions of Organisational Climate' deals with the overall view of the employees on the different dimensions of organisational climate. The perception of various dimensions of organisational climate by the employees is segregated into three levels viz., low, medium and high. An attempt has been made in this chapter to find out the impact of socio-economic factors in perception.

The fifth chapter 'Influence of Organisational Climate' presents the role of organisational climate in motivation and performance of employees. It also presents the relationship between the dimensions of organisational climate and the possession of basic job requisites.

The sixth chapter 'Preference over the different aspects of work life' gives an account of the choice made by the employees among the different aspects of work life which have an impact on organisational climate.

The seventh chapter 'Summary of findings, suggestions and conclusion' presents an overview of the findings and recommendations based on the study. The chapter also includes conclusion and suggested areas for future research in the topic chosen by the researchers.

Review of Related Literature

Introduction

This section of the study presents the review of literature of past studies on the research problem selected by the researcher. Such a review would facilitate in getting a comprehensive knowledge of the problems studied earlier and will enable the researcher to perceive, understand, adopt, modify and formulate an improved conceptual frame work for use in the current study with a view to draw meaningful and useful conclusions.

Culture Climate[1]

The culture and climate of an organisation are the natural forces which leave an imprint on the organisation. Both have strong impact on the organisation, particularly during transformation. Leaders who introduce transformation in an organisation easily be discouraged if they focus too much attention on culture alone. The management of any organisation should focus on task completion without compromising its cultural heritage. The concept of organisational climate offers a more definable and measurable vehicle for implementing change.

Culture

- Values are the ways in which individuals assess certain traits, qualities, activities or behaviours as good or bad, productive or wasteful. High levels of service, for example, might be a core value of a particular organisation. Its value might be reflected in such things as the organisation's motto, response time, reliability or actual quality and performance measurements.
- Beliefs though frequently unstated reflect an individual's understanding of the way the organisation works and the probable consequences of the actions they take. In some organsiations, people may champion new service/product ideas in the belief that innovation is the way to get ahead. In other organisations, people adhere to rules in the belief that controlling risk is the way to get ahead.
- Myths are the stories or legends that persist within the organisation.

  For example, there can be a myth surrounding the danger of taking the initiative in presenting new ideas - considered to be unwelcome. Such a story is not a piece of trivial information - it is part of a body of clues or signals that transmit what new members can or cannot do.
- Traditions are repetitive significant events such as celebrations, special awards, retirement parties and holiday dinners. These events inject predictability into the organisational environment and are a basic means of perpetuating cultural values. They highlight what is held in high esteem in the organisation.
- Norms are informal rules of the organisation regarding communication processes, dress, work habits, work hours and implicit codes of interpersonal behaviour. Does the organisation encourage open and honest communication or does it allow rumours and gossip to prevail? These 'rules of conduct' are not written down in any employee manual, but accepted as 'the way things are'.

These components are difficult and almost impossible to measure and even harder for people to articulate but they are real and have to be managed as part of the process of changing the organisation. Corporate culture in itself cannot be mandated. There are too many variables, too much out of the leader's control. It is like punching a pillow; a lot of energy is exerted but the results are transitory. Nothing seems to really change and it is difficult to determine the next best action.

Climate

Climate is the label used to describe the dimensions of the work environment that can be measured with relative precision. A variety of factors determine the climate of an organisation:

- Leadership is the single most important determinant of organisational climate in the day-to-day leadership style of the leader. The leader has a powerful influence on the expectations and behaviours of everyone in the organisation.
- Optimally, knowing how to anticipate, lead and manage change is an art. A leader needs to develop strategies to face the challenges in the future and the best ways to engage everyone in the organisation to attain the desired results. The degree in which a leader and his team address these dynamics will be reflected in the gains made.
- Organisational structure is an equally powerful determinant of climate in an organisation. The formal/informal ways through which a work is accomplished has a greater role to play in deciding the quality of climate in an organisation. The way in which an organisation conducts itself is a direct reflection of what it considers critical to its success and speaks volumes with regard to its commitment and value to its employees.

- Historical forces have a strong impact on an organisation's culture that develops over time. The circumstances surrounding the organisations's founding, the manner in which crises were faced and resolved and the organisation's role models were the important factors influencing the climate in an organisation. If an organisation was founded by individuals who have innovation in providing leading edge services, it will influence the cultural values and climate characterised by high levels of creativity. On the other hand, if the organisation has neglected innovation and resisted change, priding itself on its ability to maintain the status quo, it is predictable that when change is introduced, the impact on the organisation's culture and climate will be dramatic and most likely results in the fallout of individual's unwillingness or unable to let go.
- Standards of accountability measure the ways in which individuals take responsibility and are held accountable for both what they do and how they do it.
- Standards of behaviour are best defined in terms of what will be observed and heard. Leaders can mandate acceptable behaviours and reinforce those behaviours through a performance measurement process. For example, a desired behaviour may be treating each other with mutual respect.

  A violation of that behaviour may be observed through statements made to others, shouting and lack of co-operation. Holding people accountable for both job performance and behavioural measurements and the courage to dismiss those who do their job but violate the organisations's values, sends an important message and contributes towards the creation of desired climate.

- Communication is an important component of desired behaviour, measured by the organisation's communication patterns. Acceptable behaviours are reflected in direct, constructive and timely feedback, open communication, mutual respect and use of conflict as an asset. Lack of acceptable behaviours such as blaming others, focusing on problems rather than solutions, allowing rumours, gossip and criticisms will corrupt the corporate climate.
- Rewards measure competencies in tangible ways. Reward systems characterised by a balance of task and behavioural competencies are powerful messages. Ongoing constructive feedback offered on a quarterly basis helps to show the seriousness in achieving results and the creation of values-driven organisation.
- Trust reflects the prevailing feelings of mutual respect and support within the organisation. Trust is high when individuals sense that their input is valued, their actions are backed by others and support is direct and constructive. Trust diminishes when individuals break agreements, miss deadlines impacting others, and do not give each other the benefit of the doubt. The resultant disappointments damage trust, making it difficult to rebuild. Over time, the lack of trust has a profound negative impact on the organisation's climate and its ability to achieve its goals.
- Commitment reflects an individual's sense of pride in belonging to an organisation, and their degree of support to the future of the organisation. Strong feelings of commitment are associated with high levels of productivity, energy and action. Low levels of commitment makes change and effort difficult. Individuals feel disengaged, compliant and unwilling to participate.
- Vision and strategies are statements of the organisation's desired future. They set the context and

focus for the organisation. If any organisation has chosen an aggressive, far-reaching vision and has aligned successfully its strategies, goals, priorities and resources with its vision, the organisational culture and climate will, over time, reflect the same.

- Individuals tend to affiliate within their professions and occupations, departments and teams. As such, powerful subcultures can develop. Cutting across the organisation and bringing into alignment individuals with different points of view are essential for a healthy organisational climate. This can be done with cross-functional team projects and/or other strategies which drive inter-dependence.

External environment also influences an organisation's culture and climate. Factors such as government regulations, economic conditions, competitive industry forces and ongoing change exerts pressure on the organisation. These factors manifest themselves in different culture and climate profiles. The determinants of culture and climate provide leaders with leverage points for shaping the organisation's work environment.

Review of Literature

A.Z. Nammi and Maryam Zarra Nezhad[2] (2009) investigated the existence of relationship between components of psychological climate and organisational commitment. The study was conducted in one of the biggest cities in Iran, using a sample consisting of 170 teachers. Support was found for the existence of statistically significant relationships between psychological climate and components of organisational commitment.

Meral Elci and Lutfihak Alpkan[3] (2009) investigated the effects of nine ethical climate types viz., self-interest, company profit, efficiency, friendship, team interest, social responsibility, personal morality, company rules and professional codes on the work satisfaction of employees. The ethical climate typology developed by Victor and Cullen was tested on a sample of staff and managers from 62 different telecommunication firms in Turkey. The results obtained from the 1174 usable questionnaires confirm the existence of different ethical climate types observed in western cultures in the present sample context, which is a developing Muslim country.

Dorthe Dojbak Haakonsson *et al.* (2008)[4] in their study attempted to investigate how misalignments between the organisational climate and the leadership style may result in negative performance consequences. The result indicated that misalignment between climate and leadership style are problematic for organisational performance. Some combinations of climate and leadership style align or fit well together and yield good performance. Complementarily, there are combinations of climate and leadership style which do not fit and yield relatively poor performance.

Georgia Pashiardis[5] (2008) made an attempt to explore and analyse secondary school students' perceptions of school climate in three areas viz., the physical, social and learning environment of the school. The major findings concerning the three areas of school climate indicate that students were moderately satisfied with the climate prevailing in their school. The study revealed that the lowest mean was given to social environment, the second highest to physical environment and the highest score to learning environment. As far as the physical environment of the school is concerned, the students seem to be quite disappointed with the maintenance and cleaning of the buildings as well as the tidiness of the class rooms. The students' perception of the social environment revealed that they are generally satisfied with most of the items related to the school environment except that of a few on which they had expressed displeasure. A close observation of the students' perception on the learning environment revealed that more than fifty percent of the sample selected are satisfied.

Lawrence R. James *et al.* (2008)[6] offered a brief history of psychological climate and the product of the aggregates of psychological climate, typically referred to as 'Organisational climate'. The article begins with a synopsis of psychological climate. Discussion proceeds to organisational climate, where attention is given to what it means to form within-group aggregates of psychological climate, and what conditions these aggregates need to satisfy in order to qualify as measures of organisational climate. The relationship between climate and culture was also discussed and it was identified that the two are distinct constructs. Finally, recent research in climate is briefly summarized.

Alessia D'Amato and Fred R.H. Zijlstra[7] (2008) observed that individual characteristics of employees and the notion of cognitive regulation within situations had a prominent place. In this study, a frame work that incorporated both these aspects as determinants of work behaviour was identified and applied in research on psychological climate. Based on survey data from 406 hospital employees, a model was tested which specified organisational citizenship behaviour as a mediator of relationships between individual factors and work outcomes. The results demonstrated support for our hypothesised model of how work behaviour mediates the relationship between these antecedents and outcomes. Practical implications and future research directions were discussed.

Jeremy F. Dawson *et al.* (2008)[8] identified theoretical perspectives of climate strength, and extended these to the organisational level. The roles of climate strength were tested in 56 hospitals in the United Kingdom. Positive relationship was identified between the climate dimensions quality and integration and expert ratings of organisational performance was also identified. A curvilinear effect between climate strength and performance was also identified. A very high or very low climate strength was less beneficial than a moderate level of climate strength. However, there were no interaction effects discovered between climate and climate strength. Implications for future climate strength research are also discussed.

S. Asha[9] (2008) studied the relationship between organisational climate and employee health. Six motives of organisational climate and two employee health dimensions were measured on 69 employees in private companies, using MAO-C and Cornel Medical Index Health Questionnaire. Corrrelational analysis between climate motives and employee health dimensions had revealed that dependency climate and emotional distress are positively correlated.

James Griffith[10] (2008) examined specific aspects of organisational climate related to job satisfaction, employee turnover and organisational performance in public elementary schools. Survey data were obtained from school staff and students and from school district archives. Hypotheses tested included: (1) Employee perceptions of organisational climate and job satisfaction, when aggregated to an organisational level would represent group level constructs; (2) Employee perceptions of positive organisational climate would be associated with higher levels of job satisfaction and organisational performance with lower levels of employee turnover and (3) Relations of organisational climate to organisational performance and to employee turnover would be mediated by employee job satisfaction. The study revealed that there was no evidence for the mediating effects of organisational climate in relation to job satisfaction, employee turnover and organisational performance.

Cynthia Uline and Megan Tschannen Moran[11] (2007) in their study examined thc interplay between the quality of school facilities and student achievement. Teachers from 80 Virginia middle schools were surveyed employing measures including the school climate index, a seven item quality of school facilities scale as well as three research support items. They have examined the proposition that at least part of the explanation for the link between school building quality and student outcomes is the mediating influence of school climate. The paper also revealed that there was a close relationship between school social environment and student achievement. The social environment of school included learning climate, teacher behaviour and attitudes, principal leadership and community ties.

Dirk De Clercq and Imanol Belausteguigoitia Rius[12] (2007) in their study, examined the role of individuals' commitment in small and medium-sised firms. More specifically, the employees will commit themselves to their firm based on their current work status in the firm, their perception of the organisational climate and the firm's entrepreneurial orientation. The study also examined how individuals' commitment affect the actual effort they exert *vis-a-vis* their firm. The hypotheses of the study were tested by applying quantitative analyses to the survey data collected from 863 Mexican small and medium-sised businesses. It was found that individuals' position and tenure in the firm, their perception of psychological safety and meaningfulness, and the firm's entrepreneurial orientation were positively related to organisational commitment. A positive relationship was also found between organisational commitment and effort. Finally, the findings showed that organisational commitment mediated the relationship between many of the predictor variables and effort.

Brian Hunt and Toni Ivergard[13] (2007) stated that the government employment agency in Sweden was a key component of the national labour market focusing specifically on placing the unemployed and job-seekers in work. The agency also administered the process of providing benefits to the unemployed. The authors had described the agency, its work, some of its special features, its workforce and how these features affect organisational climate and performance. They have outlined the characteristics of a cadre organisation, particularly how features of this type of organisation influence the workplace climate. They have also discussed the ways in which workplace climate contributes to workplace performance. Finally, the authors reviewed two empirical studies of the agency and its workforce and used the data from these studies to augment their discussions.

Dangwal, R.C. *et al.* (2007)[14] analysed organisational climate, job satisfaction and managerial effectiveness in the context of pharmaceutical industry in India with special reference to Glaxo and Ranbaxy. The main objectives of this study are: (*i*) to make a comparative analysis of organisational climate, job satisfaction and managerial effectiveness in the organisations under study for the purpose of ranking, (*ii*) to interrelate age, experience and salary with organisational climate, job satisfaction and managerial effectiveness in the units and (*iii*) to make suggestions for improvements. Results and data analysis indicate that organisational climate and job satisfaction of Glaxo is more favourable with all positive subfactors and higher scores as compared to Ranbaxy. Further analysis reveals that there are such factors such as strong focus structure, responsibility, rewards, leadership and standards in Glaxo (because of highest scores obtained on these factors) as compared to Ranbaxy. This makes Glaxo more system and process oriented organisation.

Susan Carol Littell[15] (2007) explored the effect of a personality construct, hardliness and an organisational characteristic, climate, on job satisfaction and job longevity of Mid-level Nursing Managers (MLNMs). It was hypothesised that organisational climate and hardiness would be positively, moderately related to job satisfaction. It was also hypothesised that a positive but weak relationship exists between job satisfaction and longevity. The study further has a hypothesis that lack of relationship exits between demographic variables and job satisfaction. The variables were measured with Litwin and Stringer's Organisational Climate Questionnaire (OCQ), Torres' Nurse Job Satisfaction Scale, the third generation Personal Views Survey for hardiness and a questionnaire for demographic variables. A stratified, random sample of 43 hospitals were selected and the result showed that hardiness and job satisfaction were moderately correlated. The result of Pearson's correlation between satisfaction and longevity rejected the hypothesis. It was learnt that the perception of organisational climate by MLNMs has influenced their job satisfaction levels more than their hardiness. Nurse executives and other administrators must be made aware of the importance of organisational climate if we are to retain quality MLNMs.

Simberova and Zuzana[16] (2007) analysed the factors influencing approaches to learning in a firm. These factors can be divided into individual factors and factors within the firm. This paper concentrates on factors within the firm, factors of organisational culture and climate which can be modified by human resources strategy which influences learning in a positive way. The outcomes reflect the approach of the company to different employees, for example, employees before retirement do not get information about training and are not asked by managers to undergo such exercises.

Srivastav, Avinash Kumar[17] (2006) observed that organisational climate comprising three functional motives (achievement, expert influence and extension) and three dysfunctional motives (dependency, control and affiliation) was measured for 453 randomly selected respondents from a large public sector industry. Factor analysis of the six organisational climate motives or variables brought out that organisational climate is operating in the organisation in two ways. 'Larger goal orientation' and 'friendly relationship orientation' represent the two meta motives of climate prominently operating in the organisation. Generally the organisational members either focus on attaining the larger goals (making oneself relevant to others; identifying with larger goals; working for attainment of goals; striving for excellence; de-emphasizing consolidation of personal power;

undertaking responsibility instead of avoiding it) or they focus on maintaining friendly relationships (disregarding the need for expertise).

James Thomas Kunnanatt[18] (2007) studied the impact of ISO 9000 on organisational climate. This study was conducted in a 40-year old electrical engineering company operating in the state of Kerala in India. The purpose of this study was to explore how the process of ISO 9000 implementation transforms the components of organisational climate, particularly the climate motives existing in an organisation. Climate was measured both before and after the implementation of ISO 9000, using Pareek's MAO-C instrument. Based on the scores obtained for the constituent climate motives, the patterns of organisational climate that prevailed in an organisation both before and after ISO implementation were deciphered. Findings and results revealed that as a result of ISO 9000 implementation the dysfunctional organisational climate motives such as control, dependency and affiliation underwent a U-turn transformation giving way to the functional and conducive climate motives such as achievement, expert influence and extension. The findings tended to prognosticate that when implemented well the ISO 9000 system could function not just as a quality enhancement instrument but in addition as a useful tool for strategic change management that could truly hold the potential for transforming both the character and performance of organisations.

Schulte *et al.* (2006)[19] observed that both individual-level climate perceptions and organisational climate are related to job satisfaction. Using a sample of 1076 employees from 120 branches of a US-based bank, the relative importance of individual and unit-level climate on individuals' satisfaction was examined. Cross-level results of hierarchical linear models indicated that individuals' perceptions of the climate accounted for a large percentage of variance in individuals' satisfaction. Further, unit level climate systems accounted for a small but significant portion of individual satisfaction above and beyond individuals' perceptions of the climate. These results suggested that the overall climate in a work unit has some influence on individual attitudes, after accounting for individuals' idiosyncratic perceptions of the climate.

Philipa O. Idogho[20] (2006) investigated academic staff perception of organisational climate in universities in Edo State, Nigeria. The sample for the study was made up of 1025 participants drawn from three universities in Edo State. It was found out from the data that academic staff in universities in Edo State perceived the organisational climate of their institutions as favourable and there is a significant difference among academic staff in their perception. It was also learnt that academic staff do not differ in their perception of organisational climate in their institutions based on sex, age and status.

Barbara K. Townsend [21] (2006) explored the issues of what would constitute a positive organisational climate for women and minorities within the community college setting and ways in which such a climate might be achieved. The study first described some traditional or standard measures of a positive organisational climate for women and minorities and then evaluated how well the community college was doing when examined against these measures. The study also described some structural manifestations of a negative climate, including negative discourse about minorities and women, in doing so, it traces the development of some discourse patterns about these groups and provides some illustrative cultural assumptions that reflect these discourse patterns. The study concluded with implications for the community college, including some steps to be taken to improve the organisational climate for minorities and women.

Gregory A. Aarons and Angelina C. Sawitzky[22] (2006) in their study observed that staff turnover in mental health service organisations was an ongoing problem with implications on staff morale, productivity, organisational effectiveness and implementation of innovation. Recent studies in public sector services have examined the impact of organisational culture and climate on work attitudes and ultimately staff turnover. The present study examined full and partial mediation models and the effects of culture and climate on work attitudes and the subsequent impact of work attitudes on staff turnover. Multilevel structural equation models supported a partial mediation model in which organisational culture had both direct influence on work attitudes and indirect influence through organisational climate. Work attitudes significantly predicted one year staff turnover rates. These findings support the contention that both culture and climate impact work attitudes and subsequent staff turnover.

Andrew Neal *et al.* (2005)[23] examined whether the effectiveness of human resource management practices was contingent on organisational climate and competitive strategy. The concepts of internal and external fit suggests that a positive relationship between HRM and subsequent productivity will be stronger for firms with a positive organisational climate and for firms using differentiation strategies.

Malcolm G. Patterson *et al.* (2005)[24] described the development and validation of a multidimensional measure of organisational climate. The Organisational Climate Measure (OCM) was structured based on Quinn and Rohrbaugh's Competing value model. A sample of 6869 employees across 55 manufacturing organisations completed the questionnaire. The 17 scales contained within the measure had acceptable levels of reliability and were factorially distinct. Concurrent validity was measured by correlating the rating of employees with the rating of managers and it also included the descriptions of interviewers on managerial practices and organisational characteristics. Predictive validity was established using measures of productivity and innovation the measure offers researchers a relatively comprehensive and flexible approach to the assessment of organisational members' experience and promises applied and theoretical benefits.

Olukayode Ayooluwa Afolab[25] (2005) examined the influence of perceived organisational climate and locus of control on job satisfaction and turnover intentions of commercial bank workers in Benin, Edo State, Nigeria. To determine this, a 2 × 2 ANOVA was used to analyse the data. Results from the field study of 200 employees of 25 commercial banks randomly selected support the role of perceived organisational climate and locus of control on job satisfaction. The two variables also interacted to influence job satisfaction. However, only perceived organisational climate influenced turnover intentions. The results of this study suggest that when employees perceive their organisational climate favourable, their job satisfaction is increased

Malcolm Patterson *et al.* (2004)[26] observed that association between company climate and productivity would be mediated by average level of job satisfaction. In a study of 42 manufacturing companies, productivity was significantly correlated with eight aspects of organisational climate. The overall analysis showed that company productivity was more strongly correlated with those aspects of climate that had stronger satisfaction loadings. A second prediction that managers' perceptions of climate would be more closely linked to company productivity than those of non-managers was not supported. However managers' assessments of aspects of their companys' climate were significantly positive than those of non-managers.

Francisco Javier Llorens Montes *et al.* (2004)[27] studied the relationship between organisational climate and perceptions of support for innovation, considering that the relationship may be moderated by the type of labour contract the employees have with their employer. The results drawn from empirical research among 312 observations of the employees in 80 offices of a Spanish financial company enabled them to verify on the one hand, that an organisational climate characterised by support, cohesion and intrinsic recognition favors perceptions of support for innovation and on the other hand, that there are differences in the dimensions of climate that favour perceptions of support for innovation depending on the employees' contractual relationship with the organisation.

Richard M. Burton *et al.* (2004)[28] pointed out that the success of an organisation is determined by its climate, degree of trust, morale, conflict, rewards equity, leader credibility, resistance to change and scapegoating. It was also identified that organisational strategy, the firm's commitment to capital investment, innovation, quality and the like were also found to be the important determinants of firm's performance. In their study they have developed a measure of organisational climate comprised of tension, resistance to change and conflict and showed that there is a negative effect on Return on Assets (ROA).

Nwankwo, Sonny *et al.* (2004)[29] pointed out that market orientation is widely held as a credo for organisational success. Essentially, this means that organisations that are market oriented, tend to perform better than those that are not. As a result of this logic, scholars from a wide array of disciplines are showing an increasing interest in fleshing out the factors that determine organisational market orientation stances. Based on a sample drawn from the UK's Facilities management industry, this paper examined the impact of organisational climate factors on the market orientation stances of facilities management firms. The results reveal that organisational climate has a determinant influence on market orientation stances.

Michael C.G. Davidson[30] (2003) identified in his study the differences in climate and culture and examined organisational climate within the service quality framework, and how it should be incorporated into the quality initiatives. It has been identified that an overall positive organisational climate will be possible if the climate exists for service, innovation and employee welfare. Organisations need to recognise the climate for employee well being in their organisations as the basis for the development of a climate for innovation and a climate for service. It was further identified that organisational climate is affected by the prevailing organisational culture but can be measured separately by a process of scoring individuals on a climate survey and then aggregating those scores to the department and organisation as a whole.

Chris Watkin and Ben Hubbard[31] (2003) made an attempt to find out how measuring organisational climate can help leaders better understand the effect they have on motivation and performance. The authors of this research paper have presented supportive evidence as to how organisational climate can directly account for up to 30 per cent of the variance in key business performance measures. The paper suggested a model organisational climate survey which offers a catalyst for focused performance improvement. Unlike employee attitude surveys that cover a range of issues, the organisational climate survey suggested only six core dimensions viz., flexibility, responsibility, standards, rewards, clarity and team commitment that had consistently demonstrated higher direct effect on individual and work unit performance. There were practical guidelines on how to spot the early warning signs when climate starts to deteriorate, the key factors leaders need to focus on in getting it right and how climate measures can be used as a macro change lever as part of an organisational talent review.

Kristin Smith-Crowe *et al.* (2003)[32] examined organisational climate for the transfer of safety training as a moderator of relationships between safety knowledge and safety performance. Training history data, supervisory ratings of 133 hazardous waste workers' safety performance collected in two organisations in the U.S. nuclear waste industry was used as the premise. The trend in the results were consistent with the hypothesis that these relationships would be stronger in the less restrictive (more supportive) organisational climate. The implications of these findings for promoting safe work behaviours through the creation of a positive and strategically focused organisational climate for the transfer of safety training were discussed.

Maira Clark[33] (2002) pointed out that there has been an increasing interest in the field of customer retention in the last two decades. Much of that interest had focused on the economics of customer retention and developing plans and strategies for companies to follow in order to improve customer retention. There had been little research into what determines customer retention, particularly from the perspective of organisational climate. This paper examined the relationship between employees' perceptions of organisational climate and customer retention in a specific service setting, viz., a major U.K. retail bank. Employees' perceptions of the practices and procedures in relation to customer care at their branch were investigated using a case study approach. The findings revealed that there is a relationship between employees' perceptions of organisational climate and customer retention at a macro-organisational level. They suggested that organisational climate can be subdivided into five climate themes and that within each climate theme, there are several dimensions that are critical to customer retention.

Carl F. Fey and Paul W. Beamish[34] (2002) examined how organisational climate dissimilarity between parent firm and the Joint Venture Organisation (JVO) affected joint venture performance. Data were obtained through interviews with the general manager and questionnaires were completed by top-level managers from both parent firm and the Joint Venture Organisation. Results indicated that to have the best chance of success, it is important for a firm starting a joint venture, to select a partner with an organisational climate similar to its own. Results also indicated that it is important to create an organisational climate at the Joint Venture Organisation that is similar to the parent firm's organisational climate.

Roderic J.Gray[35] (2002) established a clear association between project outcomes and the climate in which those projects are implemented. Drawing on extensive field research involving project management professionals in major British organisations, project success is shown to decline as the level of personal and environmental threat perceived by project staff increases. Other organisational characteristics such as free expression, questioning, participation in the definition of goals, innovation and intrinsic satisfactions from the work itself, are all found to be positively associated with successful project outcomes, while organisational change and conflict are negatively associated with project success.

Mohammad A. Abdeen and Mahmoud A. Abu-Samra[36] (2001) aimed at determining the perceptions of Al-Quds University faculty members of its organisational climate. One hundred eighty two full-time Arabic speaking members were included in the study. A modified version of Atamneh's tool used at Yarmouk University was used and its validity and reliability were also re-determined. The results of the study showed that the faculty members had a low-ranking evaluation of the organisational climate at the University in general. Differences in their perceptions were shown with regard to sex (infavour of female), type of faculty (infavour of literary faculties), academic rank (infavour of professor) and years of experiences (infavour of those who had less than five years). Finally, improvement of organisational climate was recommended for proper university administration.

Mahn Hee Yoonern *et. al.*, (2001)[37] had examined several work climate variables and their impact on service quality. The study investigated two components for the successful implementation of excellent service performance viz., service climate and level of supportive management in the organisation. Both the climate variables are expected to affect the attitudes and behaviour of employees which consequently affect the customers' perception of employees' service performance. This study showed that the climate variables contribute directly to job satisfaction and work effort, and indirectly to an impact on customers' perception of employee service quality. The result also indicated that in addition to job satisfaction employee's work effort also played a strong, central role in determining customer's perceptions of employee service quality. The study also proposed that the climate for service as perceived by employees, influences customers' evaluation of service quality through employees' attitudinal and behavioural responses.

Roderic J. Gray[38] (2001) established a clear association between project outcomes and the social and management climate in which projects are implemented. Drawing an extensive field research involving project management professionals in major British organisations, project success was shown to decline as the level of personal and environmental threat perceived by project staff increases. Other organisational characteristics, such as free expression, questioning, participation in the definition of goals, innovation and intrinsic satisfaction from the work itself, are found to be positively associated with successful project outcomes, whilst organisational change and conflict are negatively associated with project success.

A. Neal, *et al.* (2000)[39] examined the effects of general organisational climate on safety climate and safety performance. As expected, general organisational climate exerted a significant impact on safety climate and safety climate in turn was related to self-reports of compliance with safety regulations and procedures as well as participation in safety-related activities within the workplace. The effect of general organisational climate on safety performance was mediated by safety climate, while the effect of safety climate on safety performance was partially mediated by safety knowledge and motivation.

Peter Kangis *et al.* (2000)[40] studied the link between organisational climate and its link with corporate performance. It examined the level to which 'above' and 'below' average performing companies exhibit different climate measurements. A survey was conducted on a sample of electronic component manufacturers, as a sunrise industry in a growth phase and hosiery knitwear manufacturers as a sunset industry in decline. In turn, sub samples of companies that performed above and below average for each of these sectors were selected. Climate dimension measurements collected from the staff of the sample companies were analysed against corporate performance measurements. The results showed a consistent association between climate and performance. Independently of sector, companies performing above average showed higher values on climate dimensions than those performing below average.

Mark A. Shadur *et al.* (1999)[41] have pointed out that one of the key factors that may influence employees' perceptions of involvement is organisational climate. This article examined the relationship between employee perception of involvement and the presence of organisational climate. Data were collected using a survey of 269 employees of an information technology company. The authors argued that employees involvement is composed of three essential variables, viz., participation in decision making, team work and communication. Three hierarchical regression analyses were carried out with each of the employee perception of involvement variables as a dependent variable. Employee demographic data, employee affective attitude (job satisfaction, commitment and stress) and three dimensions of organisational climate (bureaucracy, innovation and support) were entered into the regression analyses. The results showed that supportive climates and commitment significantly predicted each of the employee involvement variables. The results were related to current research literature on organisational climate and involvement, and the implications for managers were discussed.

Verbeke *et al.* (1998)[42] observed that developments within social and exact sciences take place because scientists engage in scientific practices that allow them to further expand and refine the scientific concepts within their scientific disciplines. There is disagreement among scientists as to what the essential practices are that allow scientific concepts within a scientific discipline to expand and evolve. One group looks at conceptual expansion as something that is being constrained by rational practices. Another group, however, suggests that conceptual expansion proceeds along the lines of 'everything goes.' The goal of this paper is to test whether scientific concepts expand in a rational way within the field of organisational behaviour. We will use organisational climate and culture as examples. The essence of this study consists of two core concepts: one within organisational climate and one within organisational culture. It appears that several conceptual variations are added around these core concepts. The variations are constrained by rational scientific practices. In other terms, there is evidence that the field of organisational behaviour develops rationally.

Karen Ann Grigsby[43] (1998) described schools of nursing in terms of their organisational structure and climate and the interrelationship between these factors. Triangulation of methods, including survey, interviews and field approaches were used to compare the climate in two schools of nursing that had contrasting structural features. Sixty-nine faculty and administrators participated as subjects. A theoretical, purposive sampling procedure was used to select the schools of nursing to ensure variance in the structural components of centralisation and formalization. Both schools of nursing offered bachelor and master's degrees. All faculty and administrators participated as subjects. A theoretical, purposive sampling procedure was used to select the schools of nursing offered bachelor and master's degrees. All faculty and administrators within the school of nursing were invited to participate in completing a demographic questionnaire and a climate tool. Results indicated that the two schools of nursing exhibited characteristics of both bureaucratic model and the professional model organisational structure although one organisation was more closely aligned with the professional model. Organisational climates differed in the two schools, and the school that structurally resembled the professional model had a model of more facilitative climate.

Grace Marie Dondero[44] (1997) focused his attention on how educational reform has been a persistent concern in USA for decades. Reform initiatives have focused on teacher autonomy and teacher participation in school-based decision making. Teacher autonomy leads to have a sense of ownership and empowerment where they aim to grow within their profession and to seek increased responsibility. The author believed that real education reform must provide teachers with decision making responsibility and autonomy in educational matters including choice with respect to professional development. This can only be accomplished in a supportive and nurturing organisation.

Wayne K Hoy *et al.* (1996) [45] observed that middle schools were becoming increasingly more pervasive-all but replacing traditional junior high schools. It is because they were neither elementary nor high schools, the organisational climates of middle schools were unlikely to be adequately tapped by standard measures designed for other structures. The authors had conceptualised and developed a measure of the organisational climate of middle schools and generated a typology of school climates based on openness and tested the relationship between climate and authenticity in teacher and principal behaviour. They have also observed that openness in the school climate is directly related to authenticity in teacher and principal.

McNabb *et al.* (1995)[46] conveyed that Total quality management (TQM) programs are being implemented in many government agencies with varying results. It was argued that most TQM program failures are not due to management failures but to a deep, pervasive organisational culture that engenders an operating climate which makes employees to oppose change. Government executives who are planning to implement TQM should first measure their organisation's readiness for change. If the organisational culture and climate refuse to accept change, a TQM programme will fail regardless of management's commitment to its implementation.

S. Manorama[47] (1993) has studied the impact of organisational climate on personnel management in the university libraries. The objective of the study was to find out the root cause of problems such as lack of social recognition, job dissatisfaction, under-utilisation of staff skills, and personal conflicts among the various hierarchical levels. She has identified three vital organisational factors viz., leadership process, bureaucratic principles and lack of motivational factors as responsible for the problems. The study has emphasised the need for the librarians to use highly qualified employees and to provide them with challenging jobs. Promotional avenues were identified as one of the most significant motivational factors and the libraries were found to have very less promotional chances. The study has identified the characteristics of climate as leadership process, communication pattern, motivational forces, decision making process, internal and external environment of an organisation etc., According to the study, closed or rigid climate not adapted to the environment leads to entropy. She is of the opinion that in this information age, people just do not require conventional books, but they need constructive information to solve complex problems or to take some crucial decisions. It is further added in the article that the university libraries should change their status from conventional lending libraries to a modern computerised information system which serves as a support for decision making.

Dastmalchian Ali[48] (1986) examined the relationships between organisational climate and characteristics of organisational environments. According to him, environmental characteristics include dependency, competition and uncertainty.

In addition, the relationship of climate and environments with dimensions of organisational structure and sise are examined. Using data from 15 industrial organisations in Britain, the results have shown that different environmental characteristics have different associations with organisational climate. Also, the relationships between environments and climate are not similar to those found between environments and structure. It is suggested that the creation of appropriate climates and structural design as responses to environmental pressures may be considered as complementary strategies in an attempt to maintain administrative control. The results, therefore, provide support for the suggestion that, in order to improve our understanding of the dynamics of organisational climate, characteristics of organisational environments should be incorporated into future research designs.

Ginsberg (1978)[59] has outlined how changes in climate can be planned in a systematic manner. The approach is based on an objective method of assessing performance in the area of Human Resource Management. The strategy consists of clearly defined objectives, identification of programmes to meet them and the specific actions plans for the various cost control programmes. The climate should then be surveyed on a regular basis in order to monitor progress against the plan and to assess the effectiveness of the chosen alternative.

R.W. Woodman and D.C. King[50] (1978) viewed that phenomenological organisational climate is external to the individual, yet cognitively it is internal to the level that it is affected by individual perception. Being reality-based organisational climate is capable of sharing in the sense that observers or participants may agree in their perceptions of organisational climate, although this consensus may agree in their perceptions of organisational climate, although this consensus may be constrained by individual difference in perceptions. To the level that respondents agree in their perceptions, the climate construct is considered different from job satisfaction.

A. Ross Thomas[51] (1976) in his study stated that in recent years, theorists have provided a number of schemata by which formal or complex organisations may be categorized. Although such schemes can be applied to schools, the resultant classifications have added little to one's understanding of this special type of organisation. They have not served in any significant way as catalysts for educational research. Schools are umbilical organisations and they are conceived and born of a central administrative body, but their links with such a body was never completely severed. Therefore, within education systems - local, state, national - there were to be found many similarities in the formal structure and processes of its school progeny. Nevertheless, even when schools within a system reflect closely the demands of their progenitor and achieve both the appearance and reality of a high degree of similarity, differences do exist. The organisational climate of schools is one such difference. Organisational climate is an elusive and intangible concept and yet it is one which may offer the educationalist a means of better understanding the operation of schools.

S.K. Roy and G.A. Raja[52] (1974) compared the climate of organisations in public and private sectors as seen through the eyes of the urban elite of Delhi. The public sector, as compared to the private sector was perceived to be less efficient because of nepotism, arbitrariness in union-management relations, inexperienced managers, in adequate management system and interference by Government and Political forces.

J.B.P. Sinha[53] (1973) on the basis of his study of over 800 executives of two public and two private sector organisations, found that public sector organisations are weak in terms of the following dimensions of organisational climate: promotion, efficiency, responsibility, social relationships, initiative, reward and working conditions. He has also identified poor leadership, ineffectiveness in the face of external interference, diffused reinforcement patterns and inefficiency, lack of involvement and dissatisfaction among the executives are the other problems which affect the overall work climate in public sector organisations.

Summary

The literature collected in support of the research problem chosen was reviewed in this chapter. A thorough read through of the literature collected has enabled the researcher to broaden his understanding on the research problem taken for the study. The collection of literature from journals and books has enriched the knowledge of the researcher in the subject matter of the study.

References

1. http://thekennedygroup.com
2. Nammi, A.Z. and Maryam Zarra Nezhad, 2009. 'The Relationship Between Psychological Climate and Organisational Commitment', *Journal of Applied Sciences*, Vol. 9, No. 1, pp. 161-166.
3. Elci, Meral and Lutfihak Alpkan, 2009. 'The Impact of Perceived Organisational Ethical Climate on Work Satisfaction', *Journal of Business Ethics* , Vol.84, pp. 297-311.
4. Haakonsson, Dorthe Dojbak, Richard Burton, Borge Obel, M. and Jorgen Lauridsen, 2008. 'How Failure to Align Organisational Climate and Leadership Style Affects Performance', *Management Decisions*, Vol.46, No.3, pp. 406-432.
5. Pashiardis, Georgia, 2008. 'Toward a Knowledge Base for school Climate in Cyprus's Schools', *International Journal of Education Management*, Vol. 22, No. 5, pp. 399-416.
6. James, Lawrence R., Carol C. Choi, Chia-Huei Emily Ko, Patrick K. McNeil, Matthew K. Minton, Mary Ann Wright and Kwang –il Kim, 2008. 'Organisational and Psychological Climate: A Review of Theory and Research', *European Journal of Work and Organisational Psychology,* Vol.17, No.1, pp. 5-32.

7. D'Amato, Alessia and Fred R.H. Zijlstra, 2008. 'Psychological Climate and Individual Factors as Antecedents of Work Outcomes', *European Journal of Work and Organisational Psychology* , Vol.17, No.1, pp. 33-54.
8. Dawson, Jeremy F., Vincente Gonzalez-Roma, Ann Davis and Michael A. West 2008. 'Organisational Climate and Climate Strength in UK Hospitals', *European Journal of Work and Organisational Psychology,* Vol.17, No.1, pp. 89-111.
9. Asha, S. 2008. 'Organisational Climate and Employee Health', *The ICFAI Journal of Organisational Behaviour,* Vol.7, No.1, pp. 62-65.
10. Griffith, James, 2008. 'A Compositional Analysis of the Organisational Climate-Performance Relation: Public Schools as organisations', *Journal of Applied Social Psychology,* Vol.36, No.8, pp 18-48.
11. Uline, Cynthia and Megan Tschannen Moran, 2007. 'The Walls Speak: the Interplay of Quality Facilities, School Climate and Student Achievement', *Journal of Educational Administration,* Vol. 46, No.1, pp. 55-73.
12. Clercq, Dirk De and Imanol Belausteguigoitia Rius, 2007. 'Organisational Commitment in Mexican Small and Medium Sised Firms: The Role of Work Status, organisational Climate and Entrepreneurial Orientation', *Journal of Small Business Management,* Vol.45, No.4, pp 467-490.
13. Hunt, Brian and Toni Ivergard, 2007. 'Organisational Climate and Work Place Efficiency', *Public Management Review*, Vol.9, No.1, pp.27-47.
14. Dangwal, R.C., Prof.Batra G.S., Prof. Sacher Arun, Prof. Kohli V.K., 2007. 'Organisational Climate & Managerial Effectiveness in the Pharmaceutical Sub-Sector: A Comparative Study', *Journal of Indian Management & Strategy 8M*, Vol.12, No.3, pp. 55-64.
15. Littell., Susan Carol, 2007. 'Organisational Climate and Job Satisfaction in Mid-Level Nurse Managers', *http://openlibrary.org*
16. Simberova and Zuzana, 2007. 'Factors of Organisational Climate Influencing Learning in Firms', *http://www.vet-research.net.*
17. Srivastav, Avinash Kumar, 2006. 'Organisational Climate in Public Sector: An Empirical Study', *Management & Change*, Vol.10, No.2.

18. Kunnanatt, James Thomas, 2007. 'Impact of ISO 9000 on Organisational Climate : Strategic Change Management Experience of an Indian Organisation', *International Journal of Manpower,* Vol. 28, No. 2, pp.175-195.

19. Schulte, Mathis, Ostroff, Cheri, Kinicki, Angelo, J. 2006. 'Organisational Climate Systems and Psychological Climate Perceptions: A Cross-Level Study of Climate Satisfaction Relationships', *Journal of Occupation and Organisational Psychology*, Vol.79, No.4, pp. 645-671.

20. Idogho Philipa O., 2006. 'Academic Staff Perception of the rganisational Climate in Universities in Edo State, Nigeria', *Journal of Social Sciences*, Vol.13, No.1, pp.71-78.

21. Barbara K. Townsend, 2006. 'Community College Organisational Climate for Minorities and Women', *Community College Journal of Research and Practice*, Vol.30, pp.813-826.

22. Aarons, Gregory A. and Angelina C. Sawitzky, 2006. 'Organisational Climate Partially Mediates the Effect of Culture on work Attitudes and Staff Turnover in Mental Health Services', *Administration and Policy in Mental Health and Mental Health Services Research*, Vol.33, No.3.

23. Neal, Andrew , Michael A. West and Malcolm G. Patterson, 2005. 'Do Organisational Climate and Competitive Strategy Moderate the Relationship Between Human Resources Management and Productivity', *Journal of Management,* Vol. 31, No. 4, pp. 492 – 512.

24. Patterson, Malcolm G., Michael A. West, Viv J. Shackleton, Jeremy F. Dawson, Rebecca Lawthom, Sally Maitlis, David L. Robinson and Alison M. Wallace, 2005. 'Validating the Organisational Climate Measure: Links to Managerial Practices, Productivity and Innovation', *Journal of Organisational Behaviour,* Vol.26, No.4, pp.379-408.

25. Afolab, Olukayode Ayooluwa, 2005. 'Influence of Organisational Climate and Locus of Control on Job Satisfaction and Turnover Intentions', *IFE Psychological* Vol.13, No.2, pp.102- 113.

26. Patterson, Malcolm, Peter Warr and Michael West, 2004. 'Organisational Climate and Company Productivity : The Role of Employee Affect and Employee Level', *Journal of Occupational and Organisational Psychology* , Vol.77, No.2, pp.193-216.

27. Javier, Francisco, Llorens Montes, Antonia Ruiz Moreno and Luis Miguel Molina Fernandez, 2004. 'Accessing the Organisational

Climate and Contractual Relationship for Perceptions of Support for Innovation', *International Journal of Manpower,* Vol.25, No.2, pp.167-180.

28. Burton, Richard M., Jorgen Lauridsen and Borge Obel, 2004. 'The Impact of Organisational Climate and Strategic Fit on Firm Performance', *Human Resource Management,* Vol. 43, No. 1, pp. 67-82.
29. Nwankwo, Sonny, Owusu-Frimpong, Nana, Ekwulugo and Frances, 2004. 'The Effects of Organisational Climate on Market Orientation: Evidence from the Facilities Management Industry', *Journal of Service Marketing*, Vol. 18, No. 2, pp. 122-132.
30. Michael, C.G. Davidson, 2003. 'Does Organisational Climate Add to Service Quality in Hotels?', *International Journal of Contemporary Hospitality Management*, Vol. 15, No. 4, pp. 206-213.
31. Watkin, Chris and Ben Hubbard, 2003. 'Leadership Motivation and the Drivers of Share Price : The Business Case for Measuring Organisational Climate', *Leadership and Organisation Development Journal*, Vol. 24, No. 7, pp. 380-386.
32. Kristin Smith-Crowe, Michael J. Burke and Ronald S. Landis, 2003. 'Organisational Climate as a Moderator of Safety Knowledge - Safety Performance Relationships', *Journal of Organisational Behaviour,*Vol.24, No. 7, pp. 861-876.
33. Clark, Maira, 2002. 'The Relationship Between Employees' Perceptions of Organisational Climate and Customer Retention Rates in a Major UK Retail Bank', *Journal of Strategic Marketing,* Vol. 10, pp. 93-113.
34. Carl, F. Fey and Paul W. Beamish, 2002. 'Organisational Climate Similarity and Performance: International Joint Ventures in Russia', *Organisation Studies,* Vol. 22, No.5, pp. 853-882.
35. Roderic, J. Gray, 2002. 'Organisational Climate and Project Success', *International Journal of Project Management,* Vol. 19, No.2, pp. 103-109
36. Abdeen, Mohammad A., Mahmoud A.Abu-Samra, 2001. 'The Organisational Climate at Al-Quds University as Perceived by Faculty Members: A Case Study', *An-Najah University Journal for Research-Humanities(B),* Vol.15, pp.277-309.
37. Yoonern, Mahn Hee, Sharon E. Beatty and Jaebeom Suh, 2001. 'The Effect of Work Climate on Critical Employee and Customer

Outcomes: An Employee Level Analysis', *International Journal of Service Industry Management*, Vol.12, No.5, pp. 500-521.

38. Roderic, J. Gray, 2001. 'Organisational Climate and Project Success', *International Journal of Project Management,* Vol.19, No. 2, pp. 103-109.
39. Neal, A., Griffin, M.A. and Hart, P.M. (2000). 'The impact of Organisational Climate on Safety Climate and Individual Behaviour', *Safety science* , Vol. 34, No. 1-3, pp. 99-109
40. Kangis, Peter, Gordon D. Williams.S, 2000. 'Organisational Climate and Corporate Performance: An Empirical Investigation', *Management Decision*, Vol. 38, No. 8, pp. 531-540.
41. Shadur, Mark A., Rene Kienzle and John J. Redwell, 1999. 'The Relationship Between Organisational Climate and Employee Perceptions of Involvement', *Group and Organisation Management,* Vol.24, No.4, pp. 479-503.
42. Verbeke, Willem, Volgering, Marco, Hessels, Marco, 1998. 'Exploring the Conceptual Expansion within the Field of Organisational Behaviour: Organisational Climate and Organisational Culture', Journal of Management Studies, www.faqs.org.
43. Grigsby, Karen Ann, 1998. 'The organisational Structure and Organisational Climate in two Schools of Nursing: A Comparative Analysis'.
44. Dondero, Grace Marie, 1997. 'Organisational Climate and Teacher Autonomy: Implications for Educational Reform', *International Journal of Educational Management,* Vol.11, No.5, pp. 218-221.
45. Hoy, Wayne K., James Hoffman, Dennis Sabo and James Bliss, 1996. 'The Organisational Climate of Middle Schools: The Development and Test of the OCDQ-RM', *Journal of Educational Administration,* Vol. 34, No.1, pp. 41-59.
46. McNabb, David E., Sepic, Thomas, F , 1995. 'Culture, Climate, and Total Quality Management: Measuring Readiness for Change.
47. Manorama, S, 1993. 'Impact of Organisational Climate on Personnel Management in University Libraries', *Academic Libraries,* TR Publications Private Ltd, Chennai, 1993.
48. Ali, Dastmalchian, 1986. 'Environmental Characteristics and Organisational Climate: An Exploratory Study', *Journal of* Management studies, *www.faqs.org*

49. Ginsberg, 1978. 'Strategic Planning for work Climate Modification', *Personnel Journal*, Vol.55, No.6, pp.10-20.

50. Woodman, R.W. and King, D.C., 1978. 'Organisational Climate: Science as Folklore', *Academy of Management review* , Vol. 3, pp. 816-826.

51. Ross Thomas, A. 1976. 'The Organisational Climate of Schools', *International Review of Education,* Vol. 22, No. 4, pp. 441-463.

52. Roy, S.K. and Raja, G.A. 1974. 'A Study of the Perceptions of Organisational Climate by Employees of Small Industries', *Indian Journal of Industrial Relation*, Vol. 10, No. 2, pp. 410-414.

53. Sinha, J.B.P. 1973. 'Organisational Climate and Problems of Management in India', *International Review of Applied Psychology*, Vol. 2, pp. 55-64.

3

CHAPTER

Profile of the Study Unit

Introduction

Looking back, having a close watch on the footprints and the distance travelled in the rain and shine to reach better heights, always helps to feel proud about oneself and cherish the pleasant moments that one has come acrossed in one's journey. Tracing the origin interestingly, looking at the present realistically and viewing the future optimistically enable individual and organisation to move in the right direction with enthusiasm and determination. In the present section of the study, the researcher has made an attempt to collect and present the profile related to the study area and unit. It is believed that the attempt will deepen his understanding of the working picture of the Tamil Nadu State Transport Corporation.

Tamil Nadu is in the forefront of the Indian subcontinent in providing an efficient transport service to the people. Transport facilities are a basic ingredient in a modern society for bringing people together and for the improvement of the society. The Tamil Nadu Government, with its transport corporations, provides various types of service such as metro, mofussil, express, ghat services etc., to bring the people together. Whether it rains or shines, efficient and safe transport operation is continued in all parts of Tamil Nadu by the State Transport Undertakings.

The Transport Department is having under its control 18 State Transport Undertakings including Tamil Nadu Transport Development Finance Corporation, Pallavan Transport Consultancy Services Ltd., Institute of Road Transport, Chennai and Motor Vehicles Maintenance Department.

The Transport Department is also the Nodal Agency in the State Government in respect of projects implemented by the Southern Railway, Postal and Telecommunication Department and the Civil Aviation Department of the Government of India, within the State of Tamil Nadu.

History of Tamil Nadu State Transport Corporation

In 1944 after the World War II, the British-led Central Government in India appointed a committee to analyse and report the status of public transport in the country. The committee so appointed analysed the transport system all over India and found that a majority of the private operators in the transport sector were aiming at profit maximisation only, ignoring public interest. The committee forwarded its report to the Government in 1946 recommending the nationalisation of the Transport Sector in the better interests of the nation. The Government of India then accepted the recommendations of the committee and passed an order to all the states in India to nationalise the Transport Sector.

On the basis of the order issued by the Central Government, the then Chennai Rajathani Government passed an order on 24-03-1947 to nationalise 239 private buses which were operated in Chennai, the capital of the state. As per the order of the Government, all the buses operated in Chennai were nationalised gradually before July 1948 and named as 'Government Bus Service'.

In Independent India, the States were reorganised in 1956 on the basis of the languages spoken by the people in different regions of the nation. The Karnataka and Andhra regions were segregated from the Chennai Rajathani region on the basis of the language spoken by the people and the remaining part of the region was renamed as the state of Madras. Hence the 'Government Bus Service' was changed into 'State Transport Department'.

The Kanyakumari District, which was under regime of the Tiruvithankoor State was merged with the state of Madras on 01-11-1956. The buses operated by the Tiruvithankoor state in Kanyakumari District were also merged with the State Transport Department of Chennai. The administration of Kanyakumari Transport Division was headed by a District Transport Superintendent appointed for that purpose and he was acting under the Director in Madras. The State Transport Department which was functioning in Madras and Kanyakumari entered into an agreement with the State of Karnataka and the first express transport service between Madras and Karnataka was started in August 1959. Since the operation of transport service between Madras and Karnataka was a grand success in the history of the two regions, there were enough demands from the people of the State of Madras to operate such express services locally and as a result of such popular demand, express transport service was started for locations exceeding 120 km from Madras, connecting all the district head quarters of the state. Extending the transport service in the entire region was enabled by this initiative of the Government.

The policy on Nationalisation of Transport Service which came into force in 1946 was not widely accepted in principle and it is the 'Dravida Munnetra Kalagam' (DMK) which came to power in 1967 nationalised 495 private buses without extending their permit for further operation.

The State Transport Department was divided into Chennai, Salem, Trichy and Kanyakumari for its effective functioning and four joint directors were appointed under the Director in Madras to look after the effective functioning of the departments in these four sub-regions. The state of Madras was renamed as 'Tamil Nadu' by the then Chief Minister of the State Mr. Annadurai and hence the 'State Transport Department' was renamed as 'Tamil Nadu State Transport Department'.

In 1968, the Government of Tamil Nadu appointed a high level committee to analyse the efficiency of the Tamil Nadu State Transport Department and the committee recommended that transport service should not be directly under the control of the Government and that the department might take the shape of a limited corporation. Such an initiative, it was recommended, would enable the transport sector in Tamil Nadu to function efficiently with its economic and service objectives.

The Government of Tamil Nadu on the basis of the above recommendations issued an order dated 08-11-1971 (G.O. No: 86) and the erstwhile Tamil Nadu State Transport vehicles and administration operated in Chennai and Chengalpattu were brought under the Companies Act, 1956 and named as Pallavan Transport Corporation Limited on 01-01-1972. The establishment of Pallavan Transport Corporation Limited paved the way for the inception of other corporations and there are 18 transport corporations operating at present in Tamil Nadu.

Tamil Nadu State Transport Corporation—An Overview

Tamil Nadu State Transport Corporation (TNSTC) is the Government public transport bus operator of Tamil Nadu, India. It operates buses on intra-and inter-State bus routes. It also operates on city routes. In the 2007-2008 budget it was announced that 5000 new buses would be added to the corporations within five years. TNSTC[1] is the second largest transport corporation in India and is well known for its route coverage almost to every remote area in Tamil Nadu. The TNSTC bus fare is the lowest in the country.

Tamil Nadu State Transport Corporation was the first in India to introduce excellent paintings in buses. The school students get a pass to travel in the corporation's buses at free of cost from their school to their homes. These passes are issued by the Government of Tamil Nadu. Tamil Nadu State Transport corporation operates buses of various classes to cater to different sections of the public:

1. General buses, the largest in its capacity, ply on inter district, inter-village routes and cater to a majority of the passengers.
2. Video coaches (Super Deluxe) are operated between district headquarters and to places of tourist and pilgrimage importance.
3. Ultra Deluxe coaches are operated from various important commercial centres of Tamil Nadu to Chennai, Bangalore, Thiruvanandapuram and also amongst the centres. These are the Non-AC luxury coaches of Tamil Nadu State Transport Corporation. These have recliner seats with larger leg-room, personal fans and light.
4. AC video coaches are operated from Chennai to commercial centres like Madurai, Trichy, Thanjavur, Bangalore etc. These have recliner cushion seats with personal AC vents and lights. Mineral water is available at free of cost during the journey.

The last two types of coaches are also operated by State Express Transport Corporation (SETC). Due to the sharing of market of these services and low fares, Tamil Nadu State Transport Corporation has reported losses in recent times.

Tamil Nadu Transport Corporation has its own coach building units and it uses Ashok leyland buses.

Tamil Nadu State Development Finance Corporation was established in 1972 to collect deposits from the public in order to fund Tamil Nadu State Transport Corporation.

Origin of Tamil Nadu State Transport Corporation, Tirunelveli

The Kattabomman Transport Corporation Limited (KTCL) was incorporated on 12-12-1973 and it commenced business on 1-1-1974 by taking over the assets and liabilities of the erstwhile Tamil Nadu State Transport Departments in Tirunelveli and Kanyakumari districts. Its headquarters was at Nagercoil and it covered Tirunelveli and Kanyakumari districts. The Corporation was bifurcated due to its huge sise and a new Corporation, viz., Nesamony Transport Corporation Limited was started with 352 buses with head quarters at Nagercoil and the headquarters of Kattabomman Transport Corporation Limited was shifted from Nagercoil to Tirunelveli with effect from 01-01-1983. On that date the Corporation owned 418 buses. Kattabomman Transport Corporation Limited was renamed as Tamil Nadu State Transport Corporation, (Madurai Division – II) Ltd., Tirunelveli on 1-7-1997 and its strength of buses as on 31-03-2003 was 838.

Services Available to the Public

Free Passes to Students Studying upto Standard XII

Students' free bus passes are being issued to the students studying from standard I to XII in the Government recognised schools to travel between their residence and school.

Concession Tickets Issued by the Metropolitan Transport Corporation (Chennai)

(*a*) Free-pass for students upto standard XII of recognised schools.

(*b*) 50% concession tickets & students' tokens : Students of all the Arts and Science Colleges, recognised by the Government (except Self Financing Arts & Science

Colleges), Technical Institutions (I.T.I.s, polytechnic and Engineering Colleges) and Medical Colleges could travel in buses between residence and college. The evening college and Technical Education part time students are also eligible for concession tickets from their office to College and from College to residence. In addition to this travel tokens at a cost of 70 paise each upto a maximum of 60 tokens per month can be availed for visits to specific places such as library. Cost of student concession tickets for the first 2 kms is Rs.19, upto 4 kms it is Rs.24 and upto 6 kms Rs.26 is payable every month by the students.

(*c*) Monthly Season Tickets are being sold with permission to travel 60 trips (daily 2 trips)

(*d*) Travel as you please tickets.

Holiday one-day ticket is available at Rs.30, weekly ticket at Rs.160 and Monthly ticket at Rs.600. These tickets are issued as per the conditions printed on the ticket.

Free Pass to Physically Handicapped Persons

Physically handicapped persons having a disability of 40% and above and having monthly income not exceeding Rs. 1000 are eligible for getting free pass.

Free Pass to Mentally Retarded and Blind Persons

This travel pass is issued to mentally retarded persons travelling with escorts. The disability percentage shall be 40% and above and monthly income should not exceed Rs. 1000. All blind persons having a disability percentage of 40% and above can avail themselves of this pass without age limit.

Free Pass to Freedom Fighters and their Legal Heirs/ Language Stir Participants and Cancer Patients

Freedom fighters and their legal heirs and participants in the language stir who are residents of operational area are eligible for free passes. If a cancer patient travels alone and produces a certificate from the hospital where he is treated , the conductor should collect ¼ of the journey ticket amount from the patient and should issue the actual journey ticket. The conductor will retain the certificate issued from the hospital.

Luggage Fare

Passengers can carry hand bags, small boxes upto 20 kg free of charge. The luggage fare for items meant for sale is given below :

(*a*) For vegetable basket of gunny bags up to 20 kg, minimum fare Rs. 3 or single journey fare for the distance involved whichever is higher.

(*b*) For luggage more than 20 kg minimum fare Rs. 6 or twice the journey fare whichever is higher.

(*c*) For fish basket minimum fare Rs. 8 or twice the journey fare whichever is higher.

Breakdown Service

If the operation of a bus is disturbed due to any mechanical problem, the driver of the bus will park it close to the kerb of the road without hindrance to the traffic flow.

The conductor of the bus will sign on the rear side of the tickets and stop the on coming buses and make facilities for the stranded passengers to travel further.

After transporting all the passengers, the conductor will transmit the message regarding the breakdown either to the depot or to the wireless control room. On receipt of the message the control room supervisor will send the mobile squad to attend to the repair of the vehicle and ensure that the vehicle is repaired and sent on line without delay.

In case the repair cannot be done at the breakdown spot, the bus will be taken to the depot on tow by using a lorry/ wrecker. The concerned depot will carry out the necessary repairs and send the bus on line at the earliest.

Theft / Attack / Damage to Buses

(*a*) If any passenger reports that a theft has occurred in the bus, the driver and the conductor will take the bus immediately to the nearest police station without stopping enroute and will hand over the complaint given by the passenger to the police officer. In case the theft suspects are identified, the co-operation of the passengers will be requisitioned to hand over the suspects to the police station.

(*b*) If the duty driver, conductor or passengers are attacked, efforts are to be made to handover the culprits to the nearest police station, if necessary with the help of the able bodied passengers.

(*c*) In case of an attack, the injured passenger or staff are to be taken immediately to the nearest Government hospital.

Accidents Involving State Transport Buses

(*a*) The crew of the bus should report to the Accident Branch and to the nearest police station about the location, time, accident details, route number, bus number, registration number, details of other vehicles etc., immediately.

(*b*) The injured persons should be taken immediately to the nearest Government hospital and arrangements should be made for giving medical treatment.

(*c*) The vehicle involved in the accident will be parked close to the kerb of the road without hindrance to the traffic flow after marking the wheel position of the accident vehicles.

(*d*) The driver and conductor should give a statement about the accident to the Traffic Inspector, Accident Branch of the State Transport Undertaking and also to the police. Further they should also co-operate with the investigating traffic inspector of the Accident Branch and the police in getting clues and necessary witness to investigate the accident.

(*e*) The injured persons are to be taken to the hospital immediately and in case no other vehicle is available for transportation, the injured could be taken by the same bus.

Procedure Adopted for Settling Award Amount in Accident Compensation Claims

Accident victims of the buses plied by the State Transport Undertaking buses can file a claim petition before the Motor Accident Claims Tribunal for compensation for injuries sustained by them or for the loss of life of relatives. In the event of any award being passed by the tribunal, the award amount will be deposited in the court. Motor Accident Claims Tribunal petitions are referred to lok-adalats (courts) also negotiated by the committee set up for the purpose and settled by the mutual consent of victims and the State Transport Undertaking.

Lost Property Enquiries

A passenger who loss their belongings during travel in buses may approach the P.R.O. (Public Relations Officer) over phone or through a letter with details. The loss will be enquired in detail. If the belongings are available in the office the same will be intimated to the passenger. The affected person can get back the items after submitting proper identification of the lost articles. On restoration of the articles, a small amount is collected from the passenger as storage charge and 50% of this amount will be paid to the conductor and driver who had handed over the articles at the office.

Institutes of Road Transport

The following institutions are functioning under the control of the Institute of Road Transport:

(a) *Perundurai Medical College*: In this medical college, the five and a half year M.B.B.S. programme (i.e., 4½ years study + 1 year training) is offered with a total seat of 60 out of which 40 seats are for the open quota and is filled by the Government and the remaining 20 seats are filled from among the wards of the employees of State Transport Undertakings.

(b) *Institute of Road and Transport Technology*: An automobile research oriented engineering college known as Institute of Road and Transport Technology was started in 1984 at Erode. B.E., degree courses approved by the All India Council of Technical Education offered here are Automobile Engineering, Civil Engineering, Computer Science Engineering, Mechanical Engineering, Electronics and Communication Engineering, Electrical and Electronics Engineering. The total available seats are 300, out of which 50% of the seats are for the open quota and by the Government. The remaining 50% of the seats are filled from among the wards of the employees of State Transport Undertakings. In addition, under the lateral entry scheme for three-year diploma holders, there are 30 seats out of which 50% are filled up by the Government and the remaining 50% are filled from among the wards of the employees of State Transport Undertakings. Besides the above B.E., courses, the college also conducts a three year M.C.A. course. The total seats available are 60 out of which 30 seats are filled under the open quota and the remaining 30 seats are filled from among the wards of the employees.

(c) *Polytechnics* : There are three polytechnics run by the Institute of Road Transport. They are at Chrompet (Chennai), Bargur and Tirunelveli. The Diploma courses available are Electrical and Electronics

Engineering, Electronics and Communication Engineering and Computer Technology. The total number of seats available in the three Polytechnics is 360 at the rate of 120 seats for each Polytechnic. Fifty per cent of the seats are filled under the open quota by the Principal of the concerned Polytechnics following the norms laid down by the Government and the remaining 50% seats are filled from among the wards of the employees of the State Transport Undertakings. In addition 24 seats are available for two-year diploma at each polytechnic under the lateral entry scheme. Out of the 24 seats available 12 seats are to be filled under the open quota and the remaining 12 seats under the reserved quota.

Driver Training Centres

The Institute of Road Transport is conducting three months Heavy Vehicle Driver Training course at Gummidipoondi and at the 14 Transport Corporation Training Centres for those who have passed 10th standard and are having Light Vehicle License with one year experience. The course fee is Rs. 16,200. The candidates are selected by open advertisement in newspapers.

Material Testing Laboratory, Chennai

A Material Testing Laboratory was started at the Institute of Road Transport campus to moniter the quality of the automobile components purchased by the State Transport Undertakings in Tamil Nadu. Even small scale Industries in and around Tamil Nadu manufacturing the automobile components are utilizing the testing facilities available at the Institute of Road Transport to improve the quality of their products. The automobile components are tested against ISI Standards / Manufacturers' Specifications on payment of the testing charges prescribed for each component.

Operational Features

Table 3.1 : Tamil Nadu State Transport Corporations Functioning in Tamil Nadu

Sl. No.	Name of the Corporation	Date of Operation	Principal Area of Operation
1	2	3	4
1.	Metropolitan Transport Corporation Chennai Limited	01.01.1972	Chennai Metropolitan area
2.	State Express Transport Corporation	01.04.1980	Tamil Nadu & Inter state
3.	Tamil Nadu State Transport Corporation (Villupuram Division – I)	16.01.1975	Villupuram & Cuddalore Districts
4.	Tamil Nadu State Transport Corporation (Villupuram Division – II)	01.12.1982	Vellore & Thiruvannamalai Districts
5.	Tamil Nadu State Transport Corporation (Villupuram Division – III)	01.04.1992	Kancheepuram & Thiruvallur Districts
6.	Tamil Nadu State Transport Corporation (Salem Division – I)	15.02.1973	Salem District
7.	Tamil Nadu State Transport Corporation (Salem Division – II)	01.04.1987	Dharmapuri District

(Contd.)

Table 3.1—(Contd.)

1	2	3	4
8.	Tamil Nadu State Transport Corporation (Coimbatore Division – I)	01.03.1972	Coimbatore and Nilgris Districts
9.	Tamil Nadu State Transport Corporation (Coimbatore Division – III)	01.04.1983	Erode District
10.	Tamil Nadu State Transport Corporation (Kumbakonam Division – I)	01.03.1972	Tanjore, Nagapattinam & Tiruvarur Districts
11.	Tamil Nadu State Transport Corporation (Kumbakonam Division – II)	01.04.1985	Trichy, Karur & Perambalur Districts
12.	Tamil Nadu State Transport Corporation (Kumbakonam Division – III)	01.04.1983	Karaikudi, Sivaganga & Ramanathapuram Districts
13.	Tamil Nadu State Transport Corporation (Kumbakonam Division – IV)	16.03.1996	Pudukottai
14.	Tamil Nadu State Transport Corporation (Madurai Division – I)	17.01.1972	Madurai
15.	Tamil Nadu State Transport Corporation (Madurai Division – II)	01.01.1974	Tirunelveli & Thoothukudi Districts

1	2	3	4
16.	Tamil Nadu State Transport Corporation (Madurai Division – III)	01.04.1983	Kanyakumari District
17.	Tamil Nadu State Transport Corporation (Madurai Division- IV)	01.04.1986	Dindigul District
18.	Tamil Nadu State Transport Corporation (Madurai Division –V)	01.05.1997	Virudunagar District

Source : Secondary Data.

Table 3.2 : Strength and Types of Vehicles in Tamil Nadu

Sl. No.	Year	Types of Vehicles			Total Vehicles
		Non-transport Vehicles			
		Transport Vehicles	Two Wheelers	Other Vehicles	
1.	2001-2002	4,32,106	46,00,565	6,25,426	56,58,097
2.	2002-2003	4,57,448	50,73,643	6,77,946	62,09,037
3.	2003-2004	4,72,172	55,47,755	7,32,546	67,52,473
4.	2004-2005	4,93,926	61,06,057	8,03,761	74,03,744
5.	2005-2006	5,81,106	67,50,328	8,90,296	82,21,730
6.	2006-2007	6,08,325	75,03,426	9,91,869	91,03,620
7.	2007-2008 (upto 29.2.2008)	6,90,473	82,04,528	10,93,867	99,88,868

Source : Secondary Data.

Table 3.3 : Break-up Strength of Vehicles in Tamil Nadu

Sl. No.	Transport Vehicles		Non-transport Vehicles	
1	2		3	
	Buses Used for Passenger Transportation:		**Two Wheelers:**	
1.	Buses operated by State Transport Corporations	17,874	Motor cycles	37,97,161
2.	Buses operated by the private sector	6,899	Scooters	11,96,800
3.			Mopeds	32,10,567
	Total	**24,773**	**Total**	**82,04,528**
			Other Vehicles:	
4.	Mini buses	4,002	Motor cars	8,23,427
5.			Pullers	42,110
6.	Contract vehicles	-	Tricycles	4,259

Table 3.3 (Contd.)

1	2		3	
7.	Auto rickshaws	1,44,192	Station vehicles	2,775
8.	Contract carriers	2,367	Tractors	1,22,958
9.	Tour carriers (State permit)	56,442	Three wheeler vehicles	57,683
10.	Tour Carriers (National Permit)	8,881	Four wheelers	14,567
11.	Maxicabs (State Permit)	32,865	Road Rollers	1,628
12.	Maxicabs (National Permit)	1,676	Other vehicles	24,460
13.	Omnibuses (State Permit)	423		
14.	Omnibuses (National Permit)	130		
	Total	**2,46,976**		
	Other vehicles :			
15.	Pvt. Service vehicles	7,903		
16.	School buses	10,743		
17.	Ambulances	4,104		
18	Fire fighting vehicles	1,558		
	Total	**24,308**		
	Cargo Vehicles :			
19.	Carriers (State Permit)	1,58,404		
20.	Carriers (National Permit)	38,966		
21.	Pull and Plough vehicles	61,788		
22.	Light vehicles	1,25,980		
23.	Trains	5,276		
	Total	**3,90,414**		
	Total of transport vehicles	**6,90,473**	**Total of Non-transport vehicles**	**92,98,395**
	Total number of vehicles (Col. 2 & 3)			**99,88,868**

Source : Secondary Data

Table 3.4 : Revenue Growth in the Transport Department, Tamil Nadu

Sl. No.	Revenue year	Yearly target	Vehicle tax and fare collected	Percent-age of collection	Growth rate
1.	2001-2002	651.52	651.12	99.48%	9.92%
2.	2002-2003	817.73	749.35	91.18%	14.51%
3.	2003-2004	1003.23	938.42	93.54%	25.86%
4.	2004-2005	1031.97	1018.97	98.74%	8.58%
5.	2005-2006	1137.80	1130.14	99.33%	10.91%
6.	2006-2007	1254.16	1272.69	101.47%	12.61%
7.	2007-2008	1441.00	1391.76	96.58%	9.35%

Source : Secondary Data.

Table 3.5. Steering Allowance in Tamil Nadu State Transport Corporation

Sl. No.	Steering Allowance	Distance	Amount
1.	Town Buses	Upto 150 km	4.00
		151 to 170 km	4.50
		171 to 180 km	5.00
		Over 180 km	5.50
2.	Mofussil Buses	Upto 175 km	4.25
		176 to 200 km	4.75
		201 to 225 km	5.25
		226 to 250 km	6.00
		Over 250 km	7.00
3.	Hill Station Buses	Upto 50 km	4.25
		51 to 75 km	4.75
		76 to 100 km	5.25
		101 to 125 km	6.00
		Over 125 km	7.00

Source : Secondary Data

Table 3.6 : Drivers' and Conductors' Bata and Allowances in Tamil Nadu State Transport Corporation

Sl. No.	Particulars	Amount
1.	Minimum Bata	Rs. 4.75
2.	Hill Region Collection Bata	Rs. 2.15
3.	Mofussil Region Collection Bata	Rs. 6.00
4.	Town Bus Collection Bata	Rs. 2.00
5.	Limited Stop Service Town Buses Collection Bata	Rs. 1.75
6.	Risk allowance for drivers (Single Duty)	Rs. 4.00
7.	Single Duty (Special Bata)	Rs. 7.00
8.	Night Stay Bata	Rs. 10.00
9.	Night Stay at Hill Station	Rs.11.50
10.	Night Stay at Depots	Rs.9.00
11.	Hill Allowance	Rs.3.00
12.	Night Duty Bata	Rs.11.00
13.	Night Duty Bata for Inspectors	Rs.11.50

Source : Secondary Data.

Table 3.7 : Bus Fare Per Kilometre in Tamil Nadu State Transport Corporation

Sl. No.	Category	Fare(in Rupees)
1.	Mofussil	0.28
2.	Hill Region	0.31
3.	Express	0.32
4.	Super fast	0.38
5.	Hill Region Express	0.37
6.	Hill Region ExpressSuper Deluxe	0.42
7.	Ultra Deluxe	0.52
8.	Air Conditioned	0.85
9.	Town Bus (Minimum Fare)	2
10.	Town Bus (Maximum Fare)	7

Source : Secondary Data.

Table 3.8 : Educational Institutional run by Tamil Nadu State Transport Corporation

Sl. No.	Particulars	Total seats available	Govern-ment Quota	Manage-ment Quota
1.	Perundurai Medical College	60	39	21
2.	Engineering Colleges			
	(*a*) Under-graduate Degrees in Engineering	360	234	126
	(*b*) Post-graduate Degrees in Engineering	36	18	18
	MCA Degree	60	30	30
3.	Polytechnics	520	260	260

Source : Secondary Data.

Table 3.9. Bus Utilisation in Tamil Nadu State Transport Corporation

Sl. No.	Type of Buses	Number of Buses
1.	Madras Metropolitan Buses	2775
2.	Town Buses in Districts	6072
3.	Mofussil Buses	7298
4.	State Express Buses	562
5.	State Express (Inter State) Buses	312
6.	Hill Station Buses	520
7.	Extras	1849
	Total	19,388

Source : Secondary Data.

Table 3.10. Running Efficiency of Tamil Nadu State Transport Corporation

Sl. No.	Particulars	Result
1.	Total distance covered in a year	253.83 crore km
2.	Distance covered per day	75.77 lakh km
3.	Total passengers travelling in a day	184.62 lakh
4.	Maximum revenue per day	Rs.15.29 crores

Source : Secondary Data.

Table 3.11. Diesel, Tyre and Oil Efficiency in Tamil Nadu State Transport Corporation

Sl. No.	Category	Result
1.	Metropolitan & Towns	4.80 kmpl.
2.	Mofussil	5.26 kmpl.
3.	State Express	4.93 kmpl.
4.	Hill Stations	3.97 kmpl.

Source : Secondary Data.

Table 3.12. Overtime Salary of Employees in Tamil Nadu State Transport Corporation

Sl. No.	Category	Drivers		Conductors	
		Per Hour (Rs)	Single Duty (Rs)	Per Hour (Rs)	Single Duty (Rs)
1.	Daily Rated Employees	14	-	14	-
2.	Ordinary Grade Employees	18	180	18	175
3.	Senior Grade Employees	19	190	19	185
4.	Selection Grade Employees	20	200	20	195

Source : Secondary Data.

Table 3.13 : Achievements of Drivers and the Technical Department of Tamil Nadu State Transport Corporation in Tirunelveli District

Progression in the coverage of distance per litre of diesel

Sl. No.	Year	Kilometres per litre
1.	1990 – 1991	4.28
2.	1991 – 1992	4.40
3.	1992 – 1993	4.40
4.	1993 – 1994	4.30
5.	1994 – 1995	4.20
6.	1995 – 1996	4.41
7.	1996 – 1997	4.33
8.	1997 – 1998	4.22
9.	1998 – 1999	4.24
10.	1999 – 2000	4.22
11.	2000 – 2001	4.30
12.	2001 – 2002	4.48
13.	2002 – 2003	4.61
14.	2003 – 2004	4.69
15.	2004 – 2005	4.79
16.	2005 - 2006	4.99
17.	2006 – 2007	5.13
18.	2007 – 2008	5.15

Source : Secondary Data

Awards for Low Usage of Diesel

- First place - National Award for Progression in Diesel and Oil Saving - 1995-96
- First place - National award for Progression in Diesel Saving - 2001-02
- Second place - National award for Progression in Diesel Saving - 2002-03
- First place - National award for Progression in Diesel Saving - 2004-05
- First place - National award for Progression in Diesel Saving - 2005-06

Other Related Information

Stitching Allowance for Employees

It has been learnt from the documents available that the stitching allowance for drivers and conductors is Rs.160 and Rs. 180 per pair of dress.

Cremation Assistance

The information available also shows that the family of an employee is eligible for Rs. 2,000 in the event of the death of an employee and Rs. 500 in case of the death of a family member of an employee.

Educational Assistance

The Corporation also provides educational assistance to the children of the employees. It provides a sum of Rs. 150 for two children of an employee to study upto the Higher Secondary level. The children of the deceased employees are also eligible to receive the same amount. The children of employees who pursue their studies in medicine, engineering and law are eligible to receive an educational assistance of Rs. 1,500.

Earned Leave Salary

The Corporation calculates the earned leave salary of its employees by adding the basic pay with the rest of the components of salary such as Dearness Allowance, House Rent Allowance and City Compensatory Allowance etc., in arriving at the total emoluments of the employees.

Gratuity

For an employee to become eligible to receive gratuity, he should have served in the Corporation at least for a period of five years. Death and incompetency of employees are exempted in arriving at the eligibility for receiving gratuity. An employee is eligible to receive a maximum of Rs.3.5 lakh as gratuity at the end his service in the Corporation. If an employee passes away during the course of his service, the total period of his actual service will be taken into account and the respective Transport Corporation will pay the gratuity to the family of the deceased.

Education Loan

An employee of the Corporation is eligible to avail loan for meeting the expenses in connection with the education of their children. As per the prevailing rules of the Corporation, an employee is eligible to avail loan not exceeding 50% of the total accumulation of fund in his account.

Loan for Buying a Plot / Construction of a House

An employee is eligible for availing himself of a loan to buy a plot or construct a house during the course of his employment in the Corporation. As per the existing norms the employees are eligible to avail loan up to 50% and 90% respectively out of the accumulation of fund in their provident fund account for buying a plot or constructing a house.

Marriage Loan

Marriage is an auspicious occasion in the life of anyone and the role of parents in arranging the wedding of their children cannot be ignored. The Corporation, with the view to enable the employees to get their children married, provides loan facility. Loan for marriage can be availed for three children and the maximum loan amount is Rs. 30,000. The loan has to be repaid in 35 monthly installments and the rate of interest charged on the loan is 12 per cent.

Accident-Free Award for Drivers

It has been learnt from the available information that during the year 2007-2008, 531 licenses were suspended permanently and 9165 licenses were suspended temporarily as the result of accidents leading to death of victims. In order to save the precious life of the people and to motivate the drivers to be careful with their job, the Corporation has instituted an award. As per the norms established for the award, drivers who have accident-free drive will receive a sum of Rs. 250, Rs. 275, Rs. 300, Rs. 325, Rs. 350 during the first, second, third, fourth and fifth year respectively. An additional sum of Rs.150 per year will be given to drivers for their accident-free drive exceeding five years.

New Medical Insurance Scheme

The health of employees is an asset to any organisation. In order to protect the health and well being of the employees of the corporation, the Government of Tamil Nadu has started a new Medical Insurance Scheme in association with Star Health Insurance Company (P) Limited. As per the provisions of the scheme, a sum of Rs. 25 will be deducted every month from the salary of the employees. The management of the Corporation will contribute a sum of Rs. 195 per year along with a sum of Rs. 62 towards service charge. An employee is eligible to receive medical treatment upto Rs. 2 lakh within a period of 4 years and such a facility can also be enjoyed by the children and the wife of the employee.

Summary

The various aspects related to the study area and unit were presented in this chapter. The history of Tamil Nadu State Transport Corporation, the origin of Tamil Nadu State Transport Corporation, Tirunelveli District, the services made available to the public and tables showing various subject matter of the study were presented with the view to enrich the understanding of the study area and the unit.

Perception of Organisational Climate

Introduction

The internal and the external forces influences the behaviour of an individual and the environment wherein the individual resides can not just be ignored. The overall efficiency and the involvement of an individual can either be increased or decreased depending upon the nature and the intensity of these forces. Any organisation as an entity can not create an atmosphere of its own and it is the people who are involved can create a situation which may be either conducive or non conducive to carry on their work more interestingly and productively. More particularly, the socio-economic profile of an individual has a significant role to play in deciding the overall involvement in his work and in creating a conducive atmosphere in the place of work. An attempt has been made in this section of the study to present and analyse the various socio-economic profiles of the respondents viz., age, marital status, number of dependents, work experience, nature of the job, educational qualification, salary, family status, place of living, number of earning members in the family and the total family income. A better indication of all these profile factors could help the Tamil Nadu State Transport Corporation, Madurai Division II, Tirunelveli District to build and maintain an able and committed workforce surrounded by a congenial work climate.

Socio-economic Profile of the Respondents

Age

The age of the respondent has a direct link with his ability to do the work with perfection. It also enables the respondent to act as an agent for the creation of a favourable work atmosphere in the Corporation. Table 4.1 given below presents the distribution of respondents included for the study on the basis of their age.

Table 4.1 : Distribution of Respondent by Age

Sl. No.	Age	Number of Respondents	Percentage
1.	Below 30 years	30	10
2.	31 to 40 years	105	35
3.	41 to 50 years	105	35
4.	Over 50 years	60	20
	Total	**300**	**100**

Source: Primary Data.

Table 4.1 shows that out of 300 respondents selected for the study, 30 (10%) respondents fall in below 30 years age group, 105 (35%) respondents fall in the age group of between 31 and 40 years, 105 (35%) respondents fall in the age group of between 41 and 50 years and 60 (20%) respondents fall in the age group of over 50 years.

Marital Status

The status of respondent as regards his marital position has a unique role to play in deciding his overall ability to adjust himself according to the environment in which he lives and it also increases his responsibilities as the bread winner of the family thereby enabling him to devote more time to family and work. A married respondent is expected to be more responsible and guide the youth of the work force in task accomplishment and in the creation of a better work environment. The information related to the marital status of respondents has been presented in Table 4.2.

Table 4.2 : Classification of Respondents by Marital Status

Sl. No.	Marital Status	Number of Respondents	Percentage
1.	Married	210	70
2.	Unmarried	90	30
	Total	**300**	**100**

Source: Primary Data.

It is clear from Table 4.2 that 210 (70%) respondents are married and 90(30%) respondents are unmarried in the sample population of 300 respondents.

Number of Dependents

The strength of dependents in a family increases the commitment and the seriousness with which an individual has to look after his family requirements. The employees with a higher number of dependents, through their enriched experience in family life generally help for the creation of a better work environment. Table 4.3 gives details regarding the number of dependents in the families of the respondents.

Table 4.3 : Distribution of Respondents by the Number of Dependents in the Family

Sl. No.	Marital Status	Number of Respondents	Percentage
1.	One or two	150	50
2.	Three or four	105	35
3.	Five or six	45	15
	Total	**300**	**100**

Source: Primary Data.

It is evident from Table 4.3 that out of 300 respondents selected, 150 (50%) respondents have one or two dependents in their families, 105 (35%) respondents have three or four dependents and 45 (15%) respondents have five or six dependents in their families.

Work Experience

It is experience that makes a full man. The employees in any organisation who have put in a reasonable period of service, know precisely the people, process and above all the situation in which they work. Experienced employees generally apply a refined approach in dealing with problems and thereby contribute highly towards the establishment of a good work atmosphere in the place of work. Table 4.4 gives the work experience of the respondents selected for the study.

Table 4.4 : Classification of Respondents by Work Experience

Sl. No.	Work Experience	Number of Respondents	Percentage
1.	Below 10 years	90	30
2.	11 to 20 years	75	25
3.	21 to 30 years	105	35
4.	Over 30 years	30	10
	Total	**300**	**100**

Source: Primary Data.

Table 4.4 shows that out of 300 respondents, 90 (30%) respondents have below 10 years of work experience, 75 (25%) respondents have served 11 to 20 years, 105 (35%) respondents have put in 21 years to 30 years of experience and 30 (10%) respondents have served for over 30 years.

Nature of the Job

The type of work in which an individual is involved helps him to learn more and more about the job, aspects involved in its successful completion, problems involved and methods of overcoming such problems and above all the situation prevailing in his task area. Depending upon the nature of the job, employees can either directly or indirectly become a source of influencing the environment present in their area of operation. Table 4.5 given below presents the distribution of respondents on the basis of the nature of their job.

Table 4.5 : Distribution of Respondents by Nature of Job

Sl. No.	Nature of Job	Number of Respondents	Percentage
1.	Operation of buses	180	60.0
2.	Maintenance of buses	80	26.7
3.	Office administration	40	13.3
	Total	**300**	**100**

Source: Primary Data.

One can observe from Table 4.5 that 180 (60%) respondents out of 300 respondents selected for the present study are engaged in operation of buses, 80 (26.7%) respondents are engaged in maintenance of buses and another 40 (13.3%) respondents are involved in office administrative work.

Educational Qualification

It is generally expected that a higher profile on education widens knowledge and understanding and thereby expression of behaviour that best suits the environment. The educational qualification possessed by employees shall enable them better understand and create a work environment in the process of their involvement. The educational qualification details of respondents are collected and presented in Table 4.6.

Table 4.6 : Classification of Respondents by Educational Qualification

Sl. No.	Educational Qualification	Number of Respondents	Percen-tage
1.	Diploma	45	15
2.	Degree in Engineering	15	5
3.	Upto Standard XII	120	40
4.	Degree in Arts or Science	120	40
	Total	**300**	**100**

Source: Primary Data.

It is clear from Table 4.6 given above that out of 300 respondents selected for the present study, 45 (15%) respondents are Diploma holders, 15 (5%) respondents hold a Degree in Engineering, 120 (40%) respondents have passed up to Standard XII and 120 (40%) respondents are the holders of a Degree either in Arts or Science.

Salary

The requirements believed to lead a happy or contented life are generally fulfilled through the strength of the income received by an individual. The amount of income received by an employee shall decide the level of his satisfaction, involvement, attitude to his job and above all shall contribute

Table 4.7 : Distribution of Respondents by Salary (Per Month)

Sl. No.	Salary	Number of Respondents	Percen-tage
1.	Rs.5000 – 8000	105	35
2.	Rs.8001 – 11000	90	30
3.	Rs.11001– 14000	75	25
4.	Over Rs.14000	30	10
	Total	**300**	**100**

Source: Primary Data

towards the work situation prevailing, through his contentedness. The details regarding salary received by the respondents have been collected and presented in the Table 4.7.

Table 4.7 reveals that 105 (35%) respondents draw a monthly salary between Rs.5000 and Rs.8000, 90 (30%) respondents draw a salary between Rs.8,001 and Rs.11,000, 75 (25%) respondents draw a salary between Rs.11,001 and Rs.14,000 and the remaining 30 (10%) respondents draw a monthly salary over Rs.14,000.

Family Status

The family status of an individual decides his devotion of time for the various activities. It is generally believed that employees who lead a joint family life gain more learning and adapt themselves successfully with others and thereby act as agents for the creation of a climate in the work place filled with peace and joy. The family status of respondents has been collected and given in the Table 4.8.

Table 4.8 : Classification of Respondents by Family Status

Sl. No.	Family Status	Number of Respondents	Percentage
1.	Nuclear	180	60
2.	Joint	120	40
	Total	**300**	**100**

Source : Primary Data.

Table 4.8 shows that 180 (60%) respondents live in a nuclear type of family and the remaining 120 (40%) respondents live a joint family life.

Place of Living

The availability of a person in the place of work is decided by a number of factors and one among them is the place of living.

Employees hailing from rural areas generally have to leave the work place early whereas their counterparts attending work from urban areas can spend a little more time in the place of work and thereby can contribute towards the creation of a better work environment. The information related to the place of living of the respondents is collected and given in Table 4.9.

Table 4.9 : Distribution of Respondents by Place of Living

Sl. No.	Place of Living	Number of Respondents	Percen-tage
1.	Rural	120	40
2.	Urban	180	60
	Total	**300**	**100**

Source: Primary Data

It is clear from Table 4.9 that out of 300 respondents selected for the present study, 120 (40%) respondents live in rural areas and the remaining 180 (60%) respondents live in urban areas.

Number of Earning Members in the Family

The earning members in a family are the members who earn on a daily, weekly or monthly basis. The strength of earning members decides the strength of the overall financial position of the family. Having more earning members in a family, promotes a sense of security, balance and happiness. The happiness enjoyed in the family can also be extended by employees in their place of work and thereby enhance the chance for a conducive atmosphere. The information related to the total number of earning members in the families of respondents is gathered and presented in Table 4.10.

Table 4.10 : Classification of Respondents by the Total Number of Earning Members in the Family

Sl. No.	Place of Living	Number of Respondents	Percen-tage
1.	One	120	40
2.	Two	150	50
3.	Three	30	10
	Total	**300**	**100**

Source: Primary Data

Table 4.10 shows that in the case of 120 (40%) respondents, the respondent is the sole earning member in the family. In the case of 150 (50%) another respondents, there is an additional earning member in the family apart from the respondent. In the families of the remaining 30 (10%) respondents, the total number of earning members is 3 including the respondent.

Distribution of Respondents by Total Family Income

The fulfilment of needs in a family is decided by the total family income.

The family income decides the family's spending on the various items needed for leading a happy and contented life which will enable enjoyment of a healthy family climate. Happiness in one's family will definitely reflect upon the climate in one's place of work. The details related to the total family income of the respondents are collected and presented in Table 4.11.

It is evident from Table 4.11 that out of 300 respondents selected for the study, 45 (15%) respondents have a total family income below Rs. 10,000, 75 (25%) respondents have a family income ranging between Rs.10,001 and

Rs. 16,000,120 (40%) respondents have a total family income ranging between Rs. 16,001 and Rs. 22,000 and the remaining 60 (20%) respondents have a family income above Rs. 22,000.

Table 4.11 : Distribution of Respondents by Total Family Income (Per Month)

Sl. No.	Family Income	Number of Respondents	Percen-tage
1.	Below Rs. 10000	45	15
2.	Rs. 10001 to Rs. 16000	75	25
3.	Rs. 16001 to Rs. 22000	120	40
4.	Over Rs. 22000	60	20
	Total	**300**	**100**

Source: Primary Data

Cronbach's Alpha Test of Reliability

In order to establish the internal reliability of the items used under each organisational climate dimension, the researcher has conducted Cronbach's Alpha test of reliability in the present study. Cronbach's Alpha test of reliability is known for measuring the internal consistency and reliability of the items in a scale. In other words, it measures the extend to which the responses collected for a given item correlate with each other. The result of this test produces a reliability score, which is a number between 0 and 1. The reliability score increases, when the number of items in a scale increases. A higher reliability score indicates a higher reliability of the measured construct and the score exceeding 0.7 indicates a high internal reliability of the items in the scale. Table 4.12 shows the scores available for each dimension based on the data collected.

Table 4.12 : Distribution of Cronbach's Alpha Test Scores by the Dimensions of Organisational Climate

Sl.No.	Dimensions of Organisational Climate	Cronbach's Alpha Score
1.	Goal clarity and acceptance	0.758
2.	Working conditions	0.799
3.	Recognition and satisfaction	0.839
4.	Workgroup co-operation, friendliness, warmth	0.769
5.	Job importance, challenge and variety	0.857
6.	Participation and communication	0.903
7.	Rules and policies	0.836
8.	Employee commitment	0.805
9.	Conflict and pressure	0.821
10.	Fairness	0.783
11.	Opportunity for growth, innovation and change	0.609
12.	Social values and beliefs	0.870
13.	Professional and organisational esprit	0.903
14.	Management behaviour	0.904
15.	Events and celebrations	0.909
16.	Non-work related factors	0.803

Source: Primary data

It is clear from Table 4.12 that the dimension 'Goal clarity and acceptance' has obtained a reliability score of 0.758 and the dimension 'Working conditions' has the score of 0.799. The reliability score of 0.839 has been obtained by the dimension 'Recognition and satisfaction' whereas the dimension 'Work group co-operation, friendliness and warmth' has the score of 0.769. The dimension 'Job importance, challenge and variety' has the reliability score of 0.857 and the dimension 'Participation and Communication' has the score of 0.903. The score of 0.836 has been obtained by the dimension 'Rules and policies' whereas the dimension 'Employee commitment' has obtained the score of 0.805. The dimension 'Conflict and pressure' has the reliability score of 0.821 and the dimension 'Fairness' has obtained the score of 0.783. The score of 0.609 has been obtained by the dimension 'Opportunity for growth, innovation and change' whereas the dimension 'Social value and beliefs' has the score of 0.870. The dimension 'Professional and Organisational esprit' has obtained the reliability score of 0.903 and the dimension 'Management behaviour' has the score of 0.904. The score of 0.909 has been obtained by the dimension 'Events and Celebrations' whereas the dimension 'Non-work related factors' has the score of 0.803.

Table 4.13. Dimensions of Organisational Climate Profile

Sl.No.	Dimension	Description
1	2	3
1.	Goal clarity and acceptance	Goal clarity indicates the level to which the people involved in a job are clear about what is expected of them in terms of their work performance and also the awareness of the expected outcome in the functioning of an organisation. Acceptance denotes the psychological readiness of a person which is generally brought out through actions.
2.	Working conditions	The term indicates the status of the atmosphere in which a particular work is carried out.

1	2	3
3.	Recognition and satisfaction	Recognition denotes the way in which an outstanding performance is treated.Satisfaction is the contentedness of a person in an activity.
4.	Work group co-operation, friendliness and warmth	Work group co-operation denotes the mutual understanding and acceptance that the group members have in the accomplishment of a task.Work group friendliness indicates the psychological and behavioural closeness that the members of a work group enjoy in the company of others.Work group warmth indicates the amount of pleasantness with which the members of a group carry on their work.
5.	Job importance, challenge and variety.	Job importance is the relative preference given to a particular job in an array of jobs to be performed.Challenge is the readiness of a person to face difficulties in the accomplishment of a task.Variety indicates a range of preferences available for selection in accordance with the taste of a person.
6.	Participation and communication	Participation indicates the amount of physical

1	2	3
		and mental involvement extended voluntarily in an activity. Communication denotes the free transmission and exchange of information, thoughts, ideas and emotions between persons and groups.
7.	Rules and policies	Rules are a set of norms to be followed in the execution of a task or performance. Policies are standing plans or predetermined course of action that is established to guide the performance towards the organisational objectives.
8.	Employee commitment	The expression denotes the devotion and involvement with which an employee performs an activity or job.
9.	Conflict and pressure	Conflict involves the disagreement over issues and actions. Pressure is the amount of psychological and physiological compulsion exerted upon a person to carry on a particular activity.
10.	Fairness	The term refers to the application of objectivity in taking decisions concerning tasks and people.

1	2	3
11.	Opportunity for growth, innovation and change	Opportunity for growth indicates the chances made available for individuals and groups to have a vertical mobility in their job.Opportunity for innovation includes the chances extended for doing things differently from the routine. Opportunity for change involves the preferences made available to shift oneself from one activity to another.
12.	Social values and belief	Social values are a set of principles to be observed by the members of a society for its betterment. Social belief refers to the faith shared by the society on certain fundamental aspects which are necessary for its integrated development.
13.	Professional and organisational esprit	Professional esprit denotes the unity among the members practicing a particular profession. Organisational esprit refers to the unity among the members in an organisation.
14.	Management behaviour	The term implies the manner in which the members of the management respond to certain issues and deal

1	2	3
		with the situations arising in the organisation, especially relating to the work force.
15.	Events and celebrations	These are the joyous occasions that enable the people of an organisation to come close to one another and thereby find happiness in professional and personal life.
16.	Non-work related factors	They are those aspects which are not directly related to the job that one does but can influence the conditions prevailing in the organisation in general and the job in particular.

Dimensions of Organisational Climate

Organisational climate is a composition of different work related and non-work related factors present in a work environment. The composition of a climate could vary from organisation to organisation and from person to person. The differences in the respondents' perception of the organisational climate present in Tamil Nadu State Transport Corporation, Tirunelveli District have been collected and analysed.

The researcher has used Likert's five point scaling technique for the measurement of perception. The sixteen dimensions of organisational climate listed above have six related positive statements except that of the sixteenth one, each used for eliciting the opinion of the respondents on every dimension. The respondents were asked to mark their opinion on a five point scale consisting of the items:

Strongly Agree (SA), Agree (A), Undecided (UD), Disagree (DA) and Strongly Disagree (SDA). The scale items carry the values 5, 4, 3, 2 and 1 respectively. The total score for each statement under each dimension was calculated by multiplying the number of respondents in a scale with its respective value. The total score secured by each statement shows its significance in relation to the other statements included under each dimension. The dimensions and the statements included, the total score obtained by each scale and statement and the grand total score of all the statements have been shown in Tables from 4.13 to 4.28. The core aspect covered in the statements included in the questionnaire has been denoted as Focus of statement in the table.

Goal Clarity and Acceptance

Knowing ahead of doing by an individual develops better understanding of what is really expected of him. Awareness of an employee on what is actually expected of him in a job and his willingness to do the job enables him to decide on the time, method and the effort to be devoted for its effective accomplishment. Such awareness and willingness in the employees produce a congenial work environment. The details relating to the perception of the respondents on Goal clarity and acceptance are gathered and given in Table 4.13.

Table 4.13 shows the overall score obtained by each of the statements given under the dimension goal clarity and acceptance. The perception of employees on the statement that work expectations are properly understood by the employees has obtained a score of 1031 whereas the statement that work allotted is within the reach of the employees has the score of 701. The perception of respondents on the statement that clarity in work enables the timely completion of the work has secured a score of 808 and the statement that clarity in work given increases job effectiveness has obtained a score of 789. The statement that the role of employees' performance in organisational goal attainment has been

Table 4.13. Respondents' Perception of Goal Clarity and Acceptance

Sl.No.	Focus of Statements	Types of Response and Score					Total
		SDA	DA	UD	A	SA	Score
1.	Work expectations are properly understood by the employees	15	88	306	292	330	1031
2.	Work allotted is within the reach of the employees	77	216	225	68	115	701
3.	Clarity in work enables the timely completion of the work	19	304	189	136	160	808
4.	Clarity in work given increases job effectiveness	21	242	348	128	50	789
5.	The role of employees' performance in the attainment of organisational goal has been understood properly	17	244	348	120	75	804
6.	Clarity in work given increases perfection in work completion	19	210	309	240	65	843
	Total	**168**	**1304**	**1725**	**984**	**795**	**4976**

Source: Primary data.

understood properly has a score of 804 whereas the statement that clarity in work given increases perfection in work completion, has secured a score of 843. It can also be observed that the overall score of all the statements under this dimension is 4976.

Working Conditions

The role of individual and situational factors in job related behaviour of employees is always important and among them the contribution of work related environment in deciding the efficiency and involvement of individuals is always significant. Knowing exactly the employees' understanding of working conditions will enable weighing the atmospheric factors and removing the impediments in carrying out a job. The details related to the respondents' perception of the working conditions are gathered and given in Table 4.14.

Table 4.14 shows that adequate facilities for ventilation, lighting etc., are provided in the work place and the statement has a total score of 805 and the statement that work duration and timings are suitable and encouraging has secured a score of 631. The perception of employees on the statement that the work given is adequately supported by tools, spares etc., has obtained a total score of 779 whereas the statement that sufficient first aid care is provided in the work place in case of emergency, has a score of 748. The understanding of respondents on the statement that work place has suitable rest, relaxation and refreshment facilities has obtained a score of 652 and the statement that buses with good working conditions are provided for passenger transportation, has secured a score of 559. It can also be observed that the overall score of all these statements under this dimension is 4174.

Recognition and Satisfaction

'Children will cry for recognition and men will die for recognition' is a famous quote which emphasizes the need

Table 4.14. Respondents' Perception of Working Condition

Sl.No.	Focus of Statements	Types of Response and Score					Total
		SDA	DA	UD	A	SA	Score
1.	Adequate facilities for ventilation , lighting etc., are provided in the work spot	47	146	369	168	75	805
2.	Work duration and timings are suitable and encouraging the employees	122	174	135	120	80	631
3.	Work given is adequately supported by tools, spares etc.,	44	212	276	172	75	779
4.	Sufficient first aid care is provided in the work place in case of emergency	45	236	321	16	130	748
5.	Work place has suitable rest, relaxation and refreshment facilities	146	66	183	172	85	652
6.	Buses with good working condition are provided for passenger transportation	103	290	135	16	15	559
	Total	**507**	**1124**	**1419**	**664**	**460**	**4174**

Source : Primary data.

for acceptance and appreciation when people cross targeted heights in their career and personal life. Acceptance and appreciation of employees for their remarkable achievements in their job leads to fulfilment of the egoistic needs of individuals and their job satisfaction. Recognition and satisfaction lead to increased job commitment and enriched level of loyalty towards the organisation and hence the details related to the perception of the respondents on recognition and satisfaction extended to them are collected and given in Table 4.15.

Table 4.15 shows that the rewards and recognitions extended prompt the employees to do their job well and the statement has obtained a score of 686.

The statement that sufficient amount of monetary rewards are provided has a score of 777 and the statement that the superior appreciates the subordinates whenever the job is done well has secured a score of 817. A score of 854 has been obtained by the statement that the employees feel happier and proud when they are recognised by the superior and the management whereas the statement that recognitions are fairly given in the job based on the work performance, has a score of 805. The statement on satisfaction in the method of organising functions of recognition has received a score of 811. It has been further noted that the overall perception score of all the statements under this dimension is 4750.

Work Group Co-operation, Friendliness and Warmth

Any work environment surrounded by mutual love, care and concern for others always promotes faith and understanding. The right understanding of fellow employees leads to build up excellent relationships, sometimes beyond the place of work. The harmony in the workplace is largely decided by the co-operation between individuals and groups, exchange of pleasantries as signs of friendliness and acceptance and the warmth extended and enjoyed by employees. The details of perception related to work group co-operation, friendliness and warmth among the respondents are collected and presented in Table 4.16.

Table 4.15. Respondents' Perception of Recognition and Satisfaction

Sl.No.	Focus of Statements	Types of Response and Score					Total Score
		SDA	DA	UD	A	SA	
1.	Rewards and recognitions extended by the Corporation prompt the employees to do their job well	59	264	231	112	20	686
2.	Sufficient amount of monetary rewards are provided in the job	47	176	363	116	75	777
3.	The superior appreciates the subordinates whenever the job is done well	63	114	279	296	65	817
4.	Feeling happier and proud when recognized by the superior and the management	45	186	216	172	235	854
5.	Recognitions are fairly given in the job based on the work performance	15	274	309	72	135	805
6.	Satisfaction in the method of organising functions of recognition in the Corporation	16	298	174	248	75	811
	Total	**245**	**1312**	**1572**	**1016**	**605**	**4750**

Source : Primary data

Table 4.16. Respondents' Perception of Work Group Co-operation, Friendliness and Warmth

Sl.No.	Focus of Statements	Types of Response and Score					Total
		SDA	DA	UD	A	SA	Score
1.	Pleasantness of employees in the different roles played by the supervisors as friend, guide and counselor	45	292	186	180	10	713
2.	Employees are relating one with the others as the result of trust among themselves.	77	176	270	132	60	715
3.	Subordinates are willing to approach the superiors and they are also ready to help the subordinates.	63	144	312	184	75	778
4.	Role of workgroup co-operation in work performance and satisfaction	30	326	276	48	15	695
5.	Attending family functions of superiors, subordinates etc.,	92	150	306	120	5	673
6.	Progress of friendliness and warmth among employees in the Corporation	104	176	279	44	20	623
	Total	**411**	**1264**	**1629**	**708**	**185**	**4197**

Source: Primary data.

Table 4.16 shows that the statement on pleasantness of employees in different roles played by the superiors has received a score of 713 and the statement that employees are relating with the others as the result of the trust among themselves has secured a score of 715. The statement on subordinates' willingness to approach the superiors and their readiness to help the subordinates has obtained a score of 778 whereas the statement on the role of workgroup co-operation in work performance and satisfaction has a score of 695. The respondents' perception of the statement that they are attending the family functions of their superiors and subordinates has obtained a score of 673 and the statement that they find progress in friendliness and warmth among themselves has secured a score of 623. The overall score of all the statements under this dimension is 4197.

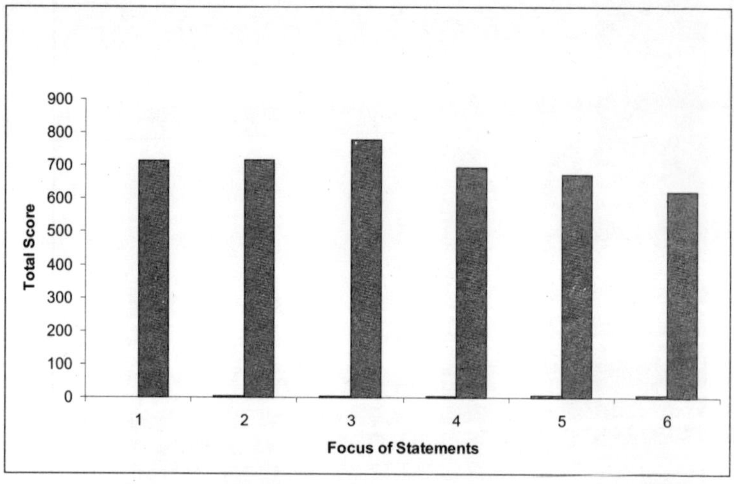

Fig. 4.1. Respondents' Perception of work Group Co-operation, Friendliness and Warmth

Job Importance, Challenge and Variety

The relative worth of a man in an organisation is decided by the position that he occupies in the organisational ladder. Higher achievers always prefer to face risk and challenge in their virgin job attempts to prove innovation and creativity and such people always will avoid doing the same job again and again all through their life time.

The real feel of employees on the job they actually perform is of paramount importance as it leads to satisfaction in their job and thereby to a conducive organisational environment for people and to increased productivity. The details related to the respondents' perception of job importance, challenge and variety are gathered and given in Table 4.17.

Table 4.17 presents the respondents' perception of the statement that the job is challenging and it demands skill and experience with an intensity value of 716 and the statement that the work allotted to employees motivates their performance has a score of 682. The statement that variety in job develops interest in performance has obtained a score of 662 whereas the statement that new jobs produce excitement and result in improved learning has secured a score of 678. A score of 707 has been obtained by the statement that variety in job helps to prove the self worth of employees and the statement that challenge in jobs leads to creativity and innovation in work has received a score of 620. The overall perception score of all the statements under this dimension is 4065.

Participation and Communication

Collective wisdom is always better than individual wisdom as it enables a thorough scrutiny of issues by a group throwing open the pros and cons on the subject matter for decision. Apart from gaining perfection in decisions, working together always produces pleasant feelings and promotes a sense of understanding and acceptance. Above all, a free exchange of opinions, ideas about people, processes etc., enables people to know each other and thereby creates an atmosphere of cordiality and warmth. The details related to the respondents' perception of participation and communication in their work place are collected and presented in Table 4.18.

Table 4.17. Respondents' Perception of Job Importance, Challenge and Variety

Sl.No.	Focus of Statements	Types of Response and Score					Total
		SDA	DA	UD	A	SA	Score
1.	Job is challenging and it demands skill and experience	75	180	279	112	70	716
2.	The work allotted to employees motivates their performance	74	242	174	172	20	682
3.	Variety in job develops interest in performance	32	424	93	48	65	662
4.	New jobs produce excitement and result in improved learning	61	268	216	128	5	678
5.	Variety in job helps to prove the self worth of employees	15	388	186	108	10	707
6.	Challenge in job leads to creativity and innovation in work	73	332	93	112	10	620
	Total	**330**	**1834**	**1041**	**680**	**180**	**4065**

Source : Primary data.

Table 4.18. Respondents' Perception of Participation and Communication

Sl.No.	Focus of Statements	Types of Response and Score					Total Score
		SDA	DA	UD	A	SA	
1.	Superior welcomes the suggestions of subordinates about the job	62	356	87	112	15	632
2.	Belated communication given by the management does not affect personal work	17	328	228	128	55	756
3.	Participative decision making indicates the recognition extended and the respect for self-worth	73	214	309	8	75	679
4.	Corporation acts as a role model for participative decision making	90	272	87	104	95	648
5.	Communication is received clearly, precisely and in time	64	276	228	72	20	660
6.	Employee participation in decision making of the Corporation is a reality	45	298	186	164	15	708
	Total	**351**	**1744**	**1125**	**588**	**275**	**4083**

Source : Primary data.

Table 4.18 shows the respondents' perception of the statement that the superior welcomes the suggestions of subordinates in the job and the same has a score of 632 whereas the statement that belated communication given does not affect personal work has secured an intensity value of 756. A score of 679 has been obtained for the statement that participative decision making indicates recognition and respect for self-worth and the statement that Corporation acts as a role model for participative decision making has received a score of 648. An intensity value of 660 has been obtained for the statement that communication is received clearly, precisely and in time whereas the statement that employee participation in decision making of the Corporation is a reality has a score of 708. The table also shows that the overall intensity value of all the statements under this dimension is 4083.

Rules and Policies

The success of an organisation is partially determined by the co-operation extended by its workforce in implementing the rules and policies as visualised by its promoters. The adherence of rules and policies by the work force in an organisation depends on how they weigh the same in terms of its relevance to promote orderliness and achieve the end results. The prevailing rules and policies always have a role in deciding the level of warmth enjoyed by the people in an organisation. The details related to the respondents' perception of the rules and policies of the Corporation are collected and presented in Table 4.19.

It is clear from Table 4.19 that the respondents' perception of the statement that the rules and regulations of the Corporation are applied impartially and the same carries an intensity value of 619 whereas the respondents' perception of the statement that the rules and regulations are inconsistent with the modern age has the score 622. The respondents' perception of existing rules and regulations in promoting orderliness, justice etc., carries an intensity value of 598 and

Table 4.19. Respondents' Perception of Rules and Politics

Sl.No.	Focus of Statements	Types of Response and Score					Total Score
		SDA	DA	UD	A	SA	
1.	Rules and regulations of the Corporation are applied impartially	77	296	168	68	10	619
2.	Rules and regulations are inconsistent with the modern age	103	242	132	60	85	622
3.	Existing rules and regulations promote orderliness, ensures justice and develops interest in performance etc.,	105	268	96	64	65	598
4.	Recruitment policy ensures availability of skilled work force	4	352	213	176	25	770
5.	Recruitment policy ensures a balanced distribution of employment opportunity for all	31	214	354	128	60	787
6.	Promotions are not given on the basis of recommendations from higher-ups or employee unions	61	182	360	72	50	725
	Total	**381**	**1554**	**1323**	**568**	**295**	**4121**

Source : Primary data.

the statement that the recruitment policy of the Corporation ensures the availability of skilled workforce has received a score of 770. The respondents' perception of the role of the recruitment policy in the balanced distribution of employment opportunities to all categories of people has obtained a score of 787 whereas the perception of the statement that promotions are not given on the basis of recommendations from higher ups or employee unions and the same has secured a score of 725. It can also be observed from Table 4.19 that the overall score of all the statements under this dimension is 4121.

Employee Commitment

Devotion to God and work are always identified as good characteristics of all human beings that really make them stand distinct in whatever mission in which they are engaged. The sprout of dedication in work is a joint exercise of the individual and the organisation. The individual should accept and involve themselves in work and the organisation should also help the individuals to exhibit such characteristics. The details related to the respondents' perception of employee commitment are collected and presented in Table 4.20.

It is evident from Table 4.20 that the respondents' perception of their determination to complete the work given at any cost has a score of 677 and the statement that the commitment shown in the work has valid reasons and the same has an intensity value of 675. The respondents' perception of the source of satisfaction and whether the same is being enjoyed in the job carries a score of 607 whereas the perception statement that the commitment shown by the employees is also created by the management has obtained a score of 630. The opinion of the respondents that their commitment has made the Corporation grow has secured an intensity value of 659 and another optimistic way of looking at the progress of the commitment among the employees has a score of 614. The overall perception score of all the statements under this dimension is 3862.

Table 4.20. Respondents' Perception of Employee Commitment

Sl.No.	Focus of Statements	Types of Response and Score					Total
		SDA	DA	UD	A	SA	Score
1.	Determined to complete the work given at any cost	119	64	312	172	10	677
2.	Commitment shown in work has valid reasons	76	206	312	16	65	675
3.	Satisfaction arises out of fulfilling job commitment and the same is being enjoyed in the job	90	296	90	116	15	607
4.	Commitment shown by the employees in work is also created by the management	75	332	90	48	85	630
5.	Commitment shown by the employees in work enables the Corporation to grow	31	394	174	40	20	659
6.	Work commitment among the employees is increasing day by day	44	416	123	16	15	614
	Total	**435**	**1708**	**1101**	**408**	**210**	**3862**

Source : Primary data.

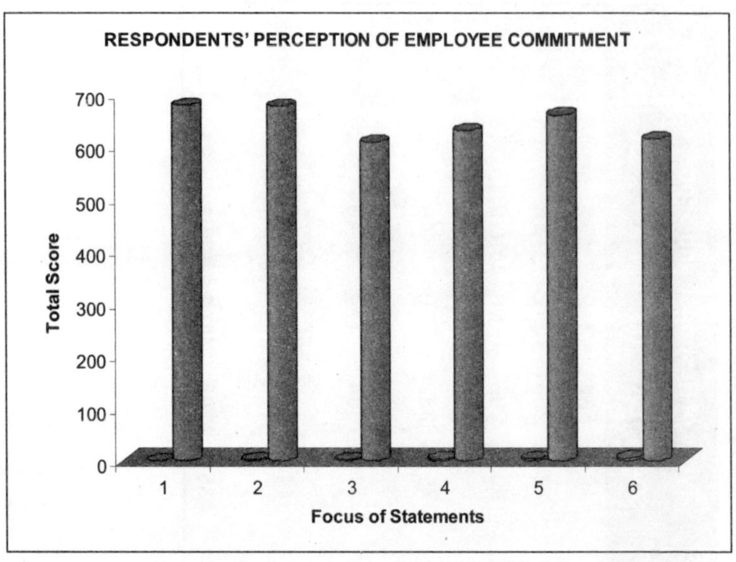

Fig. 4.2. Respondents' Perception of Employee Commitment

Work Group Conflict and Pressure

The two major bottlenecks for the happiness of individuals in their personal and work life are pressures and conflicts which are inevitable in the life of all human beings. Withstanding to conflicts and pressure becomes the source of joy or sorrow and an employee's ability to tolerate conflict and pressure is considered to be an asset for the organisation and individuals. Extended conflicts and pressure has a negative impact on the organisation and individuals. An attempt has been made to measure the views of respondents on the above subject and the details of their perception of the same has been presented in Table 4.21.

Table 4.21 shows that no pressure is exerted upon the employees in any form and the same statement carries a score of 577 whereas the statement that the work performance of employees is in accordance with the goals of the Corporation has obtained an intensity value of 781. The perception that

Table 4.21. Respondents' Perception of Conflict and Pressure

Sl.No.	Focus of Statements	Types of Response and Score					Total
		SDA	DA	UD	A	SA	Score
1.	No pressure is exerted upon the employees in the Corporation in any form	75	360	123	4	15	577
2.	Work performance of employees is in accordance with the goals of the Corporation	33	204	405	44	95	781
3.	Cordial relationship exists between superiors and subordinates	16	296	309	112	25	758
4.	Work pressure has not spoiled the relationship with fellow employees	45	420	48	56	75	644
5.	Conflict is inevitable and employees are optimistic of resolving the same	92	262	180	16	65	615
6.	Work pressure has not led to depression or sickness	180	144	9	136	55	524
	Total	**441**	**1686**	**1074**	**368**	**330**	**3899**

Source : Primary data.

there is a cordial relationship between the superiors and subordinates has a score of 758 and the statement that the prevailing work pressure has not spoiled their relationship with fellow employees has secured a score of 644. The understanding of the respondents that conflict is inevitable and the employees are optimistic of resolving the same carries a score of 615 and the perception statement that the work pressure has not led them to depression or sickness has obtained an intensity value of 524. The overall score of all the statements included under this dimension is 3899.

Fairness

Righteousness in doing things is the first step in marching towards excellence. Being fair in dealing with employees enable them to develop a positive state of mind about the work and the organisation. Any attempt of favouritism will lead to destabilise the organisational environment. The details related to the respondents' perception of fairness in the Corporation are collected and presented in Table 4.22.

Table 4.22 shows that the perception statement on the fair distribution of work among the employees has a score of 645 whereas the statement that there is no discrimination in the Corporation in providing opportunities and incentives has received an intensity value of 724. The statement that a fair treatment is extended to employees based on work performance rather than on who they are actually carries a value of 673 and the statement that fairness is objectively viewed by unions, groups etc., has secured a score of 728. The understanding of the respondents that a fair salary given increases employee satisfaction and performance carries a score of 632, whereas the perception statement that the management is fair in sharing information and resources with the employees has an intensity value of 768. It can be further observed that the overall score of all the statements under this dimension is 4170.

Table 4.22. Respondents' Perception of Fairness

Sl.No.	Focus of Statements	Types of Response and Score					Total
		SDA	DA	UD	A	SA	Score
1.	The management distributes the work fairly among the employees	101	182	222	120	20	645
2.	No discrimination is shown in the Corporation in providing opportunities and incentives	47	296	213	8	160	724
3.	Fair treatment is extended to employees						
	based on work performance rather than who they are actually	88	176	270	124	15	673
4.	Fairness is objectively viewed by unions, groups etc.,	71	124	459	4	70	728
5.	Fair salary given increases employees satisfaction and performance	90	274	129	44	95	632
6.	The Corporation is fair in sharing information and resources with the employees	60	180	309	64	155	768
	Total	**457**	**1232**	**1602**	**364**	**515**	**4170**

Source : Primary data.

Opportunity for Growth, Innovation and Change

To make the fullest use of the human potential, individuals need opportunities and organisations should provide such opportunities to bring out the skills of the work force. Engaging oneself in the same task results in boredom and monotony and hence change or rotation of job is recommended for the work force intermittently if not on a regular basis with the fullest co-operation of the individuals. An attempt has been made to collect the perception of the respondents in this regard and the same has been presented in Table 4.23.

Table 4.23 shows that opportunities are given equally among the employees to identify their latent skills and the statement has a score of 709. The statement that job rotation is encouraged among the employees has secured a score of 590 and the statement that innovation in work makes the job more interesting and effective has received an intensity value of 665. The understanding of the respondents regarding the readiness of the Corporation to bear the risks involved in creativity and innovation has obtained a score of 674 whereas the statement that the Corporation is the right place to grow and branch out has an intensity value of 694. The statement on the monetary and infrastructural support extended for innovation has received an intensity value of 663. The overall perception score of all the statements under this dimension is 3995.

Social Values and Beliefs

The way of life of individuals is largely influenced by his belief in different aspects of life coupled with the values that he has towards the people, events and happenings in the society. The values and beliefs of employees regarding the society have an impact on the life of an individual and the organisation. Any Organisational environment is surrounded by the faith of the work force in social values and their personal beliefs. The details related to the perception of respondents regarding social values and beliefs have been collected and presented in Table 4.24.

Table 4.23. Respondents' Perception of Opportunity for Growth, Innovation and Change

Sl.No.	Focus of Statements	Types of Response and Score					Total
		SDA	DA	UD	A	SA	Score
1.	Opportunities are given equally among the employees to identify their latent skills	31	326	228	104	20	709
2.	Job rotation is encouraged among the employees	60	390	123	12	5	590
3.	Innovation makes the job more interesting and effective	56	304	225	20	60	665
4.	Readiness of the Corporation to bear the risks involved in creativity and innovation	46	302	264	52	10	674
5.	Corporation is the right place to grow and branch out	48	234	393	4	15	694
6.	Innovation is suitably encouraged by monetary and infrastructural support	17	416	213	12	5	663
	Total	**258**	**1972**	**1446**	**204**	**115**	**3995**

Source : Primary data.

Table 4.24. Respondents' Perception of Social Values and Beliefs

Sl.No.	Focus of Statements	Types of Response and Score					Total
		SDA	DA	UD	A	SA	Score
1.	An egalitarian society can be created through social justice	4	82	366	412	150	1014
2.	Fundamental rights should be given to people because they are the signs of a civilised society	31	4	366	412	210	1023
3.	Ready to promote harmony in the work place.	3	82	138	532	385	1140
4.	Loyalty to parents, mentor and the society be shown	14	60	204	624	160	1062
5.	Social responsibility be shown through words and deeds	16	88	234	476	215	1029
6.	Righteousness and togetherness are still possible in this modern age	34	56	363	412	70	935
	Total	**102**	**372**	**1671**	**2868**	**1190**	**6203**

Source : Primary data.

Table 4.24 shows that the understanding of respondents regarding the creation of an egalitarian society through social justice has an intensity value of 1014 and a score of 1023 for the statement that fundamental rights ought to be given to people because they are the signs of a civilised society. The statement on the readiness of respondents to promote harmony in the work place has secured a value of 1140 whereas the perception statement that loyalty to parents, mentor and the society be shown has obtained a score of 1060. A score of 1029 has been received by the statement that social responsibility be shown through one's words and deeds and the perception statement that righteousness and togetherness are still possible in this modern age has a score of 935. The overall score of all the statements under this dimension is 6203.

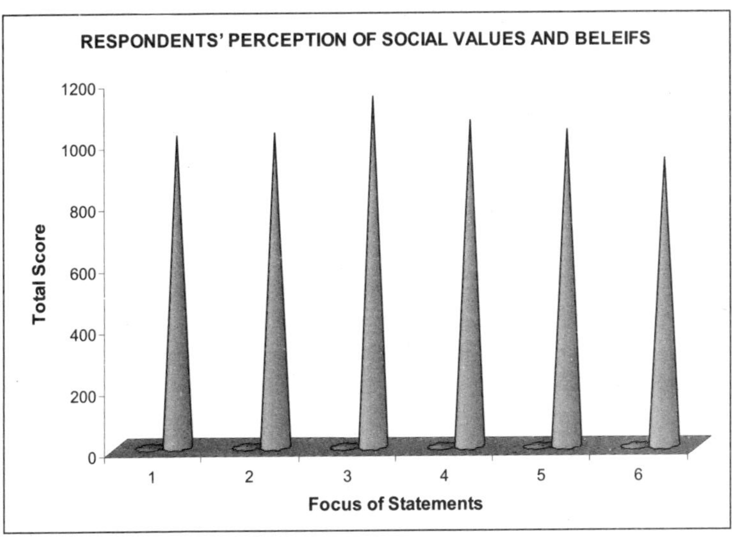

Fig. 4.3. Respondents' Perception of Social Values and Beleifs

Professional and Organisational Esprit

The major problem for the organisations of the twenty first century is bringing unity among the workforce. Feeling together is a sign of coming together and this feeling of togetherness always makes people feel confident and happier in the assignment with which they are entrusted. Professional and organisational unity enjoyed always make individuals and establishments cross better heights. An attempt has been made to collect details of the perception of respondents regarding professional and organisational esprit and the same has been presented in Table 4.25.

Table 4.25 shows the respondents' perception that unity is still possible in the work place even though diversity exists, with a score of 785 and the statement that professional esprit and organisational integration are highly related, has an intensity value of 794. The statement that work is an opportunity given and it is carried out devotedly carries a score of 920 whereas the perception statement that the overall ability of the corporation in facing competition rests in its unity, has obtained an intensity value of 893. The statement that the respondents are ready to rescue the Corporation at times of its trouble carries a score of 779 and a score of 804 for the perception statement that the Corporation will protect their interests at any cost, has an intensity value of 804. The overall perception score for all the statements under this dimension is 4975.

Management Behaviour

Healthy relationship in any organisation largely depends on the understanding of the behaviour of each other. The overall presentation of the management before its own workforce and the way in which it is looked at and interpreted decides the level of relationship among them. Any positive relationship between the management and its workforce produces happiness and a sense of satisfaction and above all it makes the entire workforce increase their involvement and commitment in their work. Such a committed workforce which finds satisfaction in the actions of the management is an asset to the organisation. The details related to the respondents' perception of management behaviour are collected and given in Table 4.26.

Table 4.25. Respondents' Perception of Professional and Organisational Esprit

Sl.No.	Focus of Statements	Types of Response and Score					Total
		SDA	DA	UD	A	SA	Score
1.	Unity is still possible in the work place even though diversity exists	15	300	303	12	155	785
2.	Professional esprit and organisational integration are highly integrated	16	266	321	116	75	794
3.	Work is an opportunity given and it is carried out devotedly	13	184	261	312	150	920
4.	The overall ability of the corporation in facing competition rests in its unity.	31	146	273	288	155	893
5.	Ready to rescue the Corporation at times of its trouble	63	144	273	284	15	779
6.	The Corporation will protect the interests of the employees at any cost	42	148	411	128	75	804
	Total	**180**	**1188**	**1842**	**1140**	**625**	**4975**

Source : Primary data.

Table 4.26. Respondents' Perception of Management Behaviour

Sl.No.	Focus of Statements	Types of Response and Score					Total
		SDA	DA	UD	A	SA	Score
1.	The Corporation is serious enough in protecting the welfare of the employees	120	270	33	132	5	560
2.	The management is not responsible for the problems in the Corporation	62	266	222	64	75	689
3.	The management's approach helps to build up the existing positive organisational climate	134	212	39	124	80	589
4.	Integrated approach of the management is the secret behind the success of the Corporation	86	292	147	60	20	605
5.	The corporation solves problems rather than involving in procrastination.	105 7	210	171	16	45	54
6.	Management is not using its power to resolve differences in issues	41	248	279	108	75	751
	Total	**548**	**1498**	**891**	**504**	**300**	**3741**

Source : Primary data.

Table 4.26 shows that there is an intensity value of 560 for the statement that the transport Corporation is serious enough in protecting the welfare of employees whereas the statement that the management is not responsible for the problems in the Corporation has received a score of 689. An intensity value of 589 has been obtained by the statement that the management's approach helps build up the existing positive organisational climate whereas the perception statement that the integrated approach of the management is the secret behind the success of the Corporation has secured a score of 605. The understanding of the respondents that the corporation solves problems immediately rather than involving in procrastination, carries a score of 547 and the statement that the management is not using its power to resolve differences in issues has an intensity value of 751. The overall score of all the statements under this dimension is 3741.

Events and Celebrations

Joyous occasions in life always make people come together, know each other and build their relationship to march together. Celebrations of auspicious occasions and festivals inside the premises of an organisation lead the workforce to forget their differences and to build an atmosphere of cordiality supported by mutual give and take. Any work environment in which its stakeholders find themselves happier is always considered as a productive environment. The details related to the perception of respondents on events and celebrations are collected and presented in Table 4.27.

Table 4.27 shows that the celebrations in the work place are the expressions of togetherness and understanding of the respondents, which carries a score of 913 whereas a score of 953 for the statement that celebration is a joyous halt in the routine to rejuvenate. The understanding of the respondents that festivals of all religions are given equal importance in the place of work carries a score of 882 and the statement

Table 4.27. Respondents' Perception of Events and Celebrations

Sl.No.	Focus of Statements	Types of Response and Score					Total
		SDA	DA	UD	A	SA	Score
1.	Celebrations in the work place are the expressions of our togetherness and understanding	16	146	363	248	140	913
2.	Celebration is a joyous halt in the routine to rejuvenate	33	26	453	296	145	953
3.	Festivals of all religions are given equal importance in the place of my work	32	214	102	404	130	882
4.	Taking active part in making arrangements for celebrations in the work place	27	156	309	188	225	905
5.	Celebrations help to close the differences with fellow employees and to work happily	13	96	402	284	170	965
6.	Staying in the place of work beyond the scheduled hours to take part in the celebrations	31	208	264	292	20	815
	Total	**152**	**846**	**1893**	**1712**	**830**	**5433**

Source : Primary data.

that the respondents are taking an active part in making arrangements for celebrations in the work place has an intensity value of 905. A score of 965 has been obtained by the perception statement that celebrations help to close the differences with fellow employees and to work happily whereas the statement showing the readiness of the respondents to stay back in the place of work beyond the scheduled hours of work to take part in the celebrations has secured a score of 815. The overall perception score of all the statements under this dimension is 5433.

Non-work Related Factors

The environment in an organisation is influenced by both internal and external factors and the role of external factors in the creation of an environment cannot be simply ignored. Employees vulnerability to external factors is always higher than internal factors because of its sensitivity. Any stock taking on the role of these factors in the creation of an internal work environment enables one to find out where exactly our labour force stands and how to make better use of these factors to build up a healthy organisational environment. The details relating to the respondents' perception of non-work related factors are collected and presented in Table 4.28.

Table 4.28 shows the perception of respondents that no difference in treatment is extended among the respondents based on caste and the same carries a score of 666 whereas the statement that alcoholism is not a problem in the transport Corporation, has an intensity value of 576.

The understanding of the respondents that the functioning of the Corporation is not affected by political interference has obtained a score of 695 and a score of 863 for the perception statement that there is no discrimination among the respondents on the basis of economical status. The understanding that discrimination is not found among the respondents on the basis of personality carries a score of 756 whereas the perception statement that there is no unethical

Table 4.28. Respondents' Perception of Non-work Related Factors

Sl.No.	Focus of Statements	Types of Response and Score					Total
		SDA	DA	UD	A	SA	Score
1.	Difference in treatment is not extended among the employees based on caste	73	244	219	120	10	666
2.	Alcoholism is not a problem in the Corporation	105	266	141	44	20	576
3.	The functioning of the Corporation is not affected by political interference	63	214	309	104	5	695
4.	Discrimination is not shown on the basis of economical status	1	200	450	132	80	863
5.	Discrimination is not shown on the basis of personality	43	214	315	164	20	756
6.	There is no unethical behaviour of individuals/ groups in the Corporation	13	334	234	112	70	763
7.	Managers and supervisors are not rude and unethical towards employees	15	204	444	128	15	806
8.	Religious affiliation has not rendered any difference in treatment among employees	32	334	213	52	85	716
9.	No use of drugs while employees are on work	64	352	135	8	65	624
10.	Employees are not under the debt trap in the Corporation	79	56	438	172	20	765
11.	Physical threat is not a problem in the Corporation	43	264	363	4	15	689
	Total	**531**	**2682**	**3261**	**1040**	**405**	**7919**

Source : Primary data

behaviour of individuals or groups in the transport Corporation, has obtained an intensity value of 763.

The understanding of the respondents that the managers and supervisors are not rude and unethical has an intensity value of 806 and the perception statement that religious affiliation of the respondents has not rendered any difference in treatment has received a score of 716. The perception of respondents that they do not use drugs while they are at work carries an intensity value of 624 whereas a score of 765 for the statement that the respondents are not under the debt trap in the transport Corporation. The understanding that physical threat is not a problem to respondents in the Corporation has an intensity value of 689. The overall score of all the twelve perception statements under this dimension is 7919.

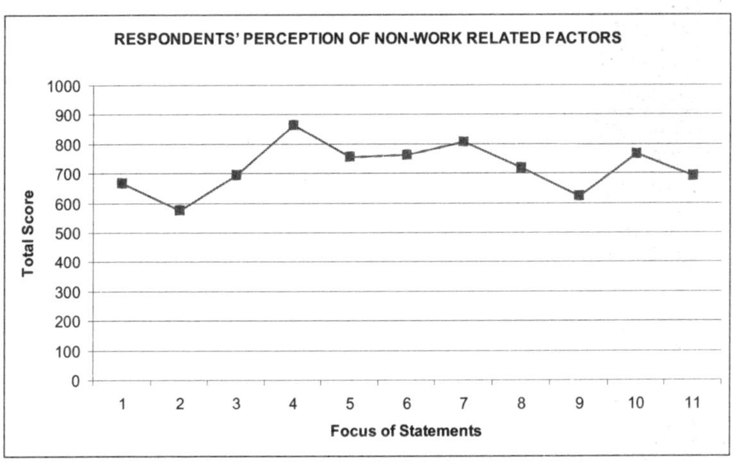

Fig. 4.4. Respondents' Perception of Non-work Related Factors

It clear from Table 4.29 that the dimension 'Non-work related factors' has the first highest mean value of 26.30 followed by the dimension 'Social values and beliefs' with the second highest mean value of 20.75. It can also be observed that the dimension 'Events and celebrations' has the third highest mean value of 18.15.

Table 4.29 : Mean and Standard Deviation of the Various Dimensions of Organisational Climate

Sl.No.	Dimension	Mean Deviation	Standard (Co-efficient of variation)	CV
1.	Goal clarity and acceptance	16.87	4.24	25.13
2.	Working conditions	13.86	4.58	33.04
3.	Recognition and satisfaction	15.85	4.79	30.22
4.	Work group co-operation, friendliness and warmth	13.95	3.97	28.46
5.	Job importance, challenge and variety	13.55	4.22	31.14
6.	Participation and communication	13.70	4.76	34.74
7.	Rules and policies	13.74	4.23	30.79
8.	Employee commitment	12.80	3.84	30.00
9.	Conflict and pressure	12.95	3.96	30.58
10.	Fairness	13.75	4.35	31.64
11.	Opportunity for growth, innovation and change	13.25	2.55	19.25
12.	Social values and beliefs	20.75	4.66	22.46
13.	Professional and organisational esprit	16.55	5.08	30.69
14.	Management behaviour	12.70	5.07	39.92
15.	Events and celebrations	18.15	5.33	29.37
16.	Non-work related factors	26.30	5.59	21.25

Source : Primary Data.

Table 4.29 also shows that the first least mean value of 12.70 has been obtained by the dimension 'Management Behaviour' followed by the second least mean value of 12.80 obtained by the dimension 'Employee commitment'. The table also reveals that the dimension 'Conflict and pressure' has the third least mean value of 12.95.

Level of Respondents' Perception of the Various Dimensions of Organisational Climate

Knowing exactly what the stakeholders of an organisation feel about different aspect helps to widen one's understanding of the people, place and process in a better manner. The enriched understanding could enable an employer to adjust, modify and effect the required changes which would enable individuals and organisations to achieve their objectives. Classification of understandings possessed by the employees of an organisation further enables the employer to remove his myth about people and understand the method in which tasks are performed. Such a classification could also enable him to remove the deviations from what is really expected of him by the employees and what is actually offered as good for their better interest in the organisation.

Given below is the classification of the respondents' perception of the various dimensions of organisational climate (Table 4.30). In order to look at the views of the respondents very closely on the different dimensions of organisational climate, the perception of the respondents has been classified into three levels viz., high, moderate and low. It has been taken for the present study that, if the overall score of a respondent for all the statements under each dimension exceeds 70% he will be considered as having a high perception towards organisational climate. On the other hand a respondent will be viewed as having a low perception towards organisational climate, if his overall score for all the statements under each dimension falls below 50%. If the overall score obtained by the respondent for all the statements under each dimension falls between 50% and 70% it will be viewed as an indicator of respondents' moderate perception.

Table 4.30 : Level of Respondents' Perception of the Various Dimensions of Organisational Climate

Sl. No.	Organisational Climate Dimensions	Low		Medium		High		Total	
		Count	%	Count	%	Count	%	Count	%
1.	Goal clarity and acceptance	153	51	72	24	75	25	300	100
2.	Working conditions	227	75.7	27	9	46	15.3	300	100
3.	Recognition and satisfaction	176	58.7	61	20.3	63	21	300	100
4.	Work group co-operation, friendliness and warmth	225	75	28	9.3	47	15.7	300	100
5.	Job importance, challenge and variety	253	84.3	4	1.3	43	14.4	300	100
6.	Participation and communication	254	84.6	4	1.3	42	14	300	100
7.	Rules and policies	257	85.7	13	4.3	30	10	300	100
8.	Employee commitment	253	84.3	19	6.3	28	9.4	300	100
9.	Conflict and pressure	268	89.3	4	1.3	28	9.4	300	100
10.	Fairness	254	84.6	4	1.3	42	14	300	100
11.	Opportunity for growth, innovation and change	252	84	33	11	15	5	300	100
12.	Social values and belief	61	20.3	29	9.7	210	70	300	100
13.	Professional and organisational esprit	184	61.3	26	8.7	90	30	300	100
14.	Management behaviour	237	79	15	5	48	16	300	100
15.	Events and celebrations	131	43.7	33	11	136	45.3	300	100
16.	Non-work related factors	240	80	29	9.7	31	10.3	300	100

Table 4.30 shows that the respondents' perception of the dimension 'Goal clarity and acceptance' has 153 (51%) respondents with a low level of perception, 72 (24%) respondents with a medium level of perception and 75 (25%) respondents with a high level of perception. The dimension 'Working conditions' has 227 (75.7%) respondents with a low level of perception, 27 (9%) respondents with a medium level of perception and 46 (15.3%) respondents with a high level of perception. It can be further noted that the respondents' perception of the dimension 'Recognition and satisfaction' has 176 (58.7%) respondents with a low level of perception, 61 (20.3%) respondents with a medium level of perception and another 63 (21%) respondents' with a high level of perception. The dimension 'Work group co-operation, friendliness and warmth' has 225 (75%) respondents with a low level of perception, 28 (9.3%) respondents with a medium level of perception and 47 (15.7%) respondents with a high level of perception.

The respondents' perception of the dimension 'Job importance, challenge and variety' has 253 (84.3%) respondents with a low level of perception, 4(1.3%) respondents with a medium level of perception and 43 (14.4%) respondents with a high level of perception. The dimension 'Participation and communication' has 254 (84.6%) respondents with a low level of perception, 4 (1.3%) respondents with a medium level of perception and 42 (14%) respondents with a high level of perception. 257 (85.7%) respondents have a low level of perception, 13 (4.3%) respondents have a medium level of perception and 30 (10%) respondents have a high level of perception of the dimension 'Rules an policies'. The respondents' perception of the dimension 'Employee commitment' has 253 (84.3%) respondents with a low level of perception, 19 (6.3%) respondents with a medium level of perception and 28 (9.4%) respondents with a high level of perception.

It could be further observed that 268 (89.3%) respondents have a low level of perception, four (1.3%) respondents have a medium level of perception and 28 (9.4%) respondents have a high level of perception of the dimension 'Conflict and pressure'. The respondents perception of 'Fairness' has 254 (84.6%) respondents with a low level of perception, 4 (1.3%) respondents with a medium level of perception and 42 (14%) respondents with a high level of perception. As far as the dimension 'Opportunity for growth, innovation and change' is concerned, 252 (84%) respondents have a low level of perception, 33 (11%) respondents have a medium level of perception and 15 (5%) respondents have a high level of perception. The dimension 'Social values and belief' has 61 (20.3%) respondents with a low level of perception, 29 (9.7%) respondents with a medium level of perception and 210 (70%) respondents with a high level of perception.

Table 4.30 above also shows that the dimension 'Professional and organisational esprit' has 184 (61.3%) respondents with a low level of perception, 26 (8.7%) respondents with a medium level of perception and 90 (30%) respondents with a high level of perception. The respondents' perception of the dimension 'Management behaviour' has 237 (79%) respondents with a low level of perception, 15 (5%) respondents with a medium level of perception and 48 (16%) respondents with a high level of perception. It could further be observed from the table given above that the dimension 'Events and celebrations' has 131(43.7%) respondents with a low level of perception, 33 (11%) respondents with a medium level of perception and 136 (45.3%) respondents with a high level of perception. The respondents' perception of 'Non-work related factors' has 240 (80%) respondents with a low level, 29 (9.7%) respondents with a medium level and 31 (10.3%) respondents with a high level of perception.

Impact of Socio-economic Factors in Perception

It is generally beleived that one's way of looking at people, process and events etc., differ from others' on the basis of internal and external aspects of life to which people are exposed. An individual has greater amount of control over internal factors such as marital status, educational qualification, place of living, family status etc., and viz., versa as for as the external forces are concerned. Coupled with a range of experience and difference in attitude towards life, employees as members of an entity could look at various developments in an organisation differently. This difference or synchronisation of views among the stakeholders of an organisation is considered to be a leading determinant in deciding the progress of an organisation. Hence an attempt has been made in this segment of the study to find out how the respondents are looking at the various core aspects of the organisation on the basis of their socio-economic conditions.

Kruscal-Wallis One-way Anova

In order to test whether there is any significant difference in the respondents' perception of the various dimensions of organisational climate with reference to age, marital status, number of dependents, work experience, nature of perception, educational qualification, salary, family status, place of living, earning members in the family and total family income, the Kruscal-Wallis One-way Anova has been used and the description of the same is as follows :

$$H = \frac{12}{N(N+1)}\left(\frac{R_1^2}{n_1} + \frac{R_2^2}{n_2} + \ldots + \frac{R_k^2}{n_k}\right) - 3(N+1)$$

Where,

$n_1, n_2, \ldots, n_k$ are the number in each of k samples

$N = n_1 + n_2 + \ldots, + n_k$ and $R_1, R_2, \ldots, R_k$. are the rank sums of each sample.

It is clear from Table 4.31 that age has a significant role to play in influencing the respondents' perception of the various dimensions of organisational climate. Significant contribution of age has been found in influencing the perception of the respondents in fifteen dimensions except the dimension 'Events and celebrations'.

Table 4.31 : Role of Age in Influencing the Respondents' Perception of the Various Dimensions of Organisational Climate

There is no significant difference in the respondents' perception of the various dimensions of organisational climate with reference to age

Sl. No.	Dimensions of Organisational Climate	'H' Value	'P' Value	Result
1.	Goal clarity and acceptance	23.473	0.000	S
2.	Working conditions	65.634	0.000	S
3.	Recognition and satisfaction	27.351	0.000	S
4.	Work group co-operation, friendliness and warmth	36.731	0.000	S
5.	Job importance, challenge and variety	38.435	0.000	S
6.	Participation and communication	67.639	0.000	S
7.	Rules and policies	31.385	0.000	S
8.	Employee commitment	26.539	0.000	S
9.	Conflict and pressure	32.095	0.000	S
10.	Fairness	94.820	0.000	S
11.	Opportunity for growth, innovation and change	14.194	0.003	S
12.	Social values and beliefs	26.083	0.000	S
13.	Professional and organisational esprit	59.696	0.000	S
14.	Management behaviour	16.934	0.001	S
15.	Events and celebrations	6.732	0.081	NS
16.	Non-work related factors	52.121	0.000	S
	Overall Score	**101.585**	**0.000**	**S**

S = Significant NS = Not Significant

The statistical data available also reveal that the calculated value of chi-square is higher than the table value (7.81) at

5 per cent level of significance. Hence, the null hypothesis is rejected. The rejection of the null hypothesis enables the researchers to conclude that the age of the respondents has influenced their perception of organisational climate.

Table 4.32 : Impact of Marital Status on Perceptual Influence

There is no significant difference in the respondents' perception of the various dimensions of organisational climate with reference to marital status.

Sl. No.	Dimensions of Organisational Climate	'H' Value	'P' Value	Result
1.	Goal clarity and acceptance	23.767	0.000	S
2.	Working conditions	110.882	0.000	S
3.	Recognition and satisfaction	14.418	0.000	S
4.	Work group co-operation, friendliness and warmth	0.028	0.867	NS
5.	Job importance, Challenge and variety	27.278	0.000	S
6.	Participation and communication	8.858	0.003	S
7.	Rules and policies	18.552	0.000	S
8.	Employee commitment	33.854	0.000	S
9.	Conflict and pressure	0.254	0.614	NS
10.	Fairness	2.206	0.137	NS
11.	Opportunity for growth, innovation and change	0.250	0.617	NS
12.	Social values and beliefs	10.978	0.001	S
13.	Professional and organisa-tional esprit	0.108	0.742	NS
14.	Management behaviour	35.650	0.000	S
15.	Events and celebrations	6.951	0.008	S
16.	Non-work related factors	6.175	0.013	S
	Overall Score	**11.627**	**0.001**	**S**

S = Significant NS = Not Significant

Table 4.32 shows that the marital status of the respondents has a role to play in influencing the respondents' perception of the various dimensions of organisational climate. The role of marital status in perceptual influence has been found in eleven dimensions out of the sixteen identified for the present study. More specifically, the marital status of the respondents has not influenced their overall perception of the dimensions, 'Work group co-operation, friendliness and warmth', 'Conflict and pressure', 'Fairness', 'Opportunity for growth, innovation and change' and 'Professional and organisational esprit'.

The information available also reveals that the calculated value of the chi-square is higher than the table value (3.84) at 5 per cent level of significance and hence the null hypothesis is rejected. The above statistical inference enables the researcher to conclude that marital status of the respondents has a role to play in influencing their perception of the various aspects of climate in the organisation.

Table 4.33 shows the role of the numerical strength of dependents in influencing the respondents' perception of organisational climate. The numerical strength of the dependents in the families of the respondents has influenced the perception of a majority of the dimensions significantly except the dimensions 'Goal clarity and acceptance', 'Work group co-operation, friendliness and warmth', 'Fairness' and 'Opportunity for growth, innovation and change'.

The statistical information available has also enabled the researcher to notice that the calculated value of the chi-square is higher than the table value (5.99) at 5 per cent level of significance and therefore the null hypothesis framed is rejected. It is clear from the rejection of the null hypothesis that the number of dependents of the respondents influences their perception of organisational climate.

Table 4.33 : Influence of the Number of Dependents on Perception

There is no significant difference in the respondents' perception of the various dimensions of organisational climate with reference to the number of dependents.

Sl. No.	Dimensions of Organisational Climate	'H' Value	'P' Value	Result
1.	Goal clarity and acceptance	2.530	0.282	NS
2.	Working conditions	10.962	0.004	S
3.	Recognition and satisfaction	20.869	0.000	S
4.	Work group co-operation, friendliness and warmth	5.432	0.066	NS
5.	Job importance, challenge and variety	36.211	0.000	S
6.	Participation and communication	28.596	0.000	S
7.	Rules and policies	51.238	0.000	S
8.	Employee commitment	33.744	0.000	S
9.	Conflict and pressure	11.315	0.003	S
10.	Fairness	4.120	0.127	NS
11.	Opportunity for growth, innovation and change	1.639	0.441	NS
12.	Social values and beliefs	47.237	0.000	S
13.	Professional and organisa-tional esprit	107.948	0.000	S
14.	Management behaviour	24.389	0.000	S
15.	Events and celebrations	31.862	0.000	S
16.	Non-work related factors	15.863	0.000	S
	Overall Score	**23.416**	**0.000**	**S**

S = Significant NS = Not Significant

Table 4.34 : Impact of Work Experience on Perception

There is no significant difference in the respondents' perception of the various dimensions of organisational climate with reference to work experience.

Sl. No.	Dimensions of Organisational Climate	'H' Value	'P' Value	Result
1.	Goal clarity and acceptance	43.574	0.000	S
2.	Working conditions	64.162	0.000	S
3.	Recognition and satisfaction	19.478	0.000	S
4.	Work group co-operation, friendliness and warmth.	60.265	0.000	S
5.	Job importance, challenge and variety	28.801	0.000	S
6.	Participation and communication	32.461	0.000	S
7.	Rules and policies	54.962	0.000	S
8.	Employee commitment	16.964	0.001	S
9.	Conflict and pressure	24.947	0.000	S
10.	Fairness	64.563	0.000	S
11.	Opportunity for growth, innovation and change	58.452	0.000	S
12.	Social values and beliefs	9.353	0.025	S
13.	Professional and organisational esprit	49.134	0.000	S
14.	Management behaviour	16.910	0.001	S
15.	Events and celebrations	24.877	0.000	S
16.	Non-work related factors	83.553	0.000	S
	Overall Score	**57.853**	**0.000**	**S**

S = Significant NS = Not Significant

Table 4.34 shows that the work experience of the respondents has played a vital role in organising their perception of the various work related aspects present in their place of work. The influence of work experience on their perception is found in all the sixteen dimensions identified for the study.

Table 4.35 : Influence of the Nature of the Job on Perception

There is no significant difference in the respondents' perception of the various dimensions of organisational climate with reference to the nature of the job.

Sl. No.	Dimensions of Organisational Climate	'H' Value	'P' Value	Result
1.	Goal clarity and acceptance	30.577	0.000	S
2.	Working conditions	34.968	0.000	S
3.	Recognition and satisfaction	1.604	0.448	NS
4.	Work group co-operation, friendliness and warmth	45.489	0.000	S
5.	Job importance, challenge and variety	2.961	0.228	NS
6.	Participation and communication	28.441	0.000	S
7.	Rules and policies	1.437	0.487	NS
8.	Employee commitment	1.149	0.563	NS
9.	Conflict and pressure	116.575	0.000	S
10.	Fairness	16.977	0.000	S
11.	Opportunity for growth, innovation and change	2.454	0.293	NS
12.	Social values and beliefs	27.368	0.000	S
13.	Professional and organisational esprit	2.513	0.285	NS
14.	Management behaviour	69.532	0.000	S
15.	Events and celebrations	75.636	0.000	S
16.	Non-work related factors	37.649	0.000	S
	Overall Score	**35.120**	**0.000**	**S**

S = Significant NS = Not Significant

The data available also reveal that the calculated value of the chi-square is higher than the table value (7.81) at 5 per cent level of significance and therefore the null hypothesis is rejected. It enables the researchers to conclude that there is an absolute influence of work experience on the respondents' perception of the various dimensions of organisational climate.

Table 4.35 shows that the nature of job has influenced the respondents' perception of organisational climate. Significant contribution of the factor is found in all the sixteen dimensions identified except the dimensions viz., 'Recognition and satisfaction', 'Job importance, challenge and variety', 'Rules and policies', 'Employee commitment', 'Opportunity for growth, innovation and change' and 'Professional and organisational esprit'.

The available statistics in the table also shows that the calculated value of the chi-square is higher than the table value (5.99) at 5 per cent level of significance. Therefore, the null hypothesis that there is no significant difference in the respondents' perception of the various dimensions of organisational climate on the basis of the nature of the job is rejected.

It is evident from Table 4.36 that the educational qualification of the respondents has an important role to play in influencing the perception of the respondents. Significant relationship has been identified between educational qualification and its influence on the perception of respondents in all the dimensions of organisational climate.

The information available also shows that the calculated value of chi-square is higher than the table value (7.81) at 5 per cent level of significance and hence the null hypothesis is rejected. It enables the researcher to conclude that educational qualification influences the respondents' perception of the organisational climate.

Table 4.36 : Impact of Educational Qualification on Perception

There is no significant difference in the respondents' perception of the various dimensions of organisational climate with reference to educational qualification.

Sl. No.	Dimensions of Organisational Climate	'H' Value	'P' Value	Result
1.	Goal clarity and acceptance	14.713	0.002	S
2.	Working conditions	42.729	0.000	S
3.	Recognition and satisfaction	8.996	0.029	S
4.	Work group co-operation, friendliness and warmth	22.102	0.000	S
5.	Job importance, challenge and variety	21.281	0.000	S
6.	Participation and communication	38.045	0.000	S
7.	Rules and policies	23.219	0.000	S
8.	Employee commitment	52.532	0.000	S
9.	Conflict and pressure	126.429	0.000	S
10.	Fairness	121.090	0.000	S
11.	Opportunity for growth, innovation and change	40.658	0.000	S
12.	Social values and beliefs	17.189	0.001	S
13.	Professional and organisational esprit	68.620	0.000	S
14.	Management behaviour	62.037	0.000	S
15.	Events and celebrations	24.741	0.000	S
16.	Non-work related factors	73.569	0.000	S
	Overall Score	**34.566**	**0.000**	**S**

S = Significant NS = Not Significant

Table 4.37 shows that the salary of the respondents has influenced their perception of organisational climate.

Table 4.37 : Influence of the Salary of the Respondents on Perception

There is no significant difference in the respondents' perception of the various dimensions of organisational climate with reference to salary.

Sl. No.	Dimensions of Organisational Climate	'H' Value	'P' Value	Result
1.	Goal clarity and acceptance	15.022	0.002	S
2.	Working conditions	7.787	0.051	NS
3.	Recognition and satisfaction	33.171	0.000	S
4.	Work group co-operation, friendliness and warmth	61.072	0.000	S
5.	Job importance, challenge and variety	16.743	0.001	S
6.	Participation and communication	35.247	0.000	S
7.	Rules and policies	50.405	0.000	S
8.	Employee commitment	20.729	0.000	S
9.	Conflict and pressure	60.705	0.000	S
10.	Fairness	75.332	0.000	S
11.	Opportunity for growth, innovation and change	50.411	0.000	S
12.	Social values and beliefs	15.411	0.001	S
13.	Professional and organisational esprit	37.806	0.000	S
14.	Management behaviour	7.368	0.061	NS
15.	Events and celebrations	38.214	0.000	S
16.	Non-work related factors	104.172	0.000	S
	Overall Score	**22.878**	**0.000**	**S**

S = Significant NS = Not Significant

Out of the sixteen dimensions identified, the salary received by the respondents has shown a significant impact on fourteen dimensions. More specifically, the salary of the respondents has not influenced their perception of the dimensions 'Working conditions' and 'Management Behaviour'.

The statistical information available also shows that the calculated value of the chi-square is higher than the table value (7.81) at 5 per cent level of significance and hence the null hypothesis framed is rejected. It enables the researcher to conclude that the salary received by the respondents influences their perception of the various core elements present in the organisation that contribute towards the prevailing work climate.

Table 4.38 shows that the family status of the respondents has played a unique role in influencing their perception. 'Goal clarity and acceptance', 'Conflict and pressure', 'Social values and belief' are the dimensions on which the family status of the respondents has not extended any significant impact and the signs of significant impact are evident in all the other core aspects of organisational climate.

The statistical data available shows that the calculated value of the chi-square is less than the table value (3.84) at 5 per cent level of significance. Since the calculated value is less than the table value, the null hypothesis is accepted. It enables the researcher to conclude that the family status of the respondents does not influence their perception of the various dimensions of organisational climate.

Table 4.39 shows the role of 'Place of living' in influencing the perception of the respondents. Significant impact of the place of living is found in eight dimensions out of the sixteen identified. 'Goal clarity and acceptance', 'Recognition and satisfaction', 'Work group co-operation, friendliness and warmth', 'Job importance, challenge and variety', 'Participation and communication', 'Employee commitment', 'Fairness', 'Social values and beliefs' and 'Events and celebrations' are the dimensions on which the place of living of the respondents has extended significant impact.

Table 4.38 : Impact of Family Status on Perception

There is no significant difference in the respondents' perception of the various dimensions of organisational climate with reference to family status.

Sl. No.	Dimensions of Organisational Climate	'H' Value	'P' Value	Result
1.	Goal clarity and acceptance	1.680	0.195	NS
2.	Working conditions	56.872	0.000	S
3.	Recognition and satisfaction	8.609	0.003	S
4.	Work group co-operation, friendliness and warmth	19.257	0.000	S
5.	Job importance, challenge and variety	9.935	0.002	S
6.	Participation and communication	52.843	0.000	S
7.	Rules and policies	10.725	0.001	S
8.	Employee commitment	4.087	0.043	S
9.	Conflict and pressure	2.986	0.084	NS
10.	Fairness	6.100	0.014	S
11.	Opportunity for growth, innovation and change	51.528	0.000	S
12.	Social values and beliefs	0.216	0.642	NS
13.	Professional and organisational esprit	4.632	0.031	S
14.	Management behaviour	12.733	0.000	S
15.	Events and celebrations	6.082	0.014	S
16.	Non-work related factors	4.707	0.030	S
	Overall Score	**2.821**	**0.093**	**NS**

S = Significant NS = Not Significant

The information available also shows that the calculated value of the chi-square is higher than the table value (3.84) at 5 per cent level of significance and hence the null hypothesis is rejected. The rejection of the hypothesis framed enables the researcher to conclude that the place of living of the respondents influences their perception of the various dimensions of organisational climate.

Table 4.39 : Influence of Place of Living on Perception

There is no significant difference in the respondents' perception of the various dimensions of organisational climate with reference to the place of living

Sl. No.	Dimensions of Organisational Climate	'H' Value	'P' Value	Result
1.	Goal clarity and acceptance	25.840	0.000	S
2.	Working conditions	2.400	0.121	NS
3.	Recognition and satisfaction	27.569	0.000	S
4.	Work group co-operation, friendliness and warmth	47.554	0.000	S
5.	Job importance, challenge and variety	41.751	0.000	S
6.	Participation and communication	32.749	0.000	S
7.	Rules and policies	1.945	0.163	NS
8.	Employee commitment	7.835	0.005	S
9.	Conflict and pressure	1.209	0.271	NS
10.	Fairness	0.000	1.000	NS
11.	Opportunity for growth, innovation and change	0.609	0.435	NS
12.	Social values and beliefs	15.009	0.000	S
13.	Professional and organisational esprit	1.158	0.282	NS
14.	Management behaviour	0.024	0.877	NS
15.	Events and celebrations	30.789	0.000	S
16.	Non-work related factors	1.537	0.215	NS
	Overall Score	**9.354**	**0.002**	**S**

S = Significant NS = Not Significant

Table 4.40 shows the role.of the earning members in the family of the respondents in influencing their perception of the various dimensions of organisational climate.

Table 4.40 : Impact of the Earning Members in the Family of the Respondents on Perception

There is no significant difference in the respondents' perception of the various dimensions of organisational climate with reference to the number of earning members in the family

Sl. No.	Dimensions of Organisational Climate	'H' Value	'P' Value	Result
1.	Goal clarity and acceptance	38.428	0.000	S
2.	Working conditions	32.323	0.000	S
3.	Recognition and satisfaction	62.318	0.000	S
4.	Work group co-operation, friendliness and warmth.	97.847	0.000	S
5.	Job importance, challenge and variety	11.195	0.004	S
6.	Participation and communication	33.876	0.000	S
7.	Rules and policies	13.476	0.001	S
8.	Employee commitment	21.113	0.000	S
9.	Conflict and pressure	14.290	0.001	S
10.	Fairness	50.615	0.000	S
11.	Opportunity for growth, innovation and change	37.477	0.000	S
12.	Social values and beliefs	80.294	0.000	S
13.	Professional and organisational esprit	50.728	0.000	S
14.	Management behaviour	0.878	0.645	NS
15.	Events and celebrations	51.031	0.000	S
16.	Non-work related factors	15.261	0.000	S
	Overall Express	**129.772**	**0.000**	**S**

S = Significant NS = Not Significant

It can be observed from Table 4.40 that no significant impact of the earning members in the family of the respondents is found in the dimension 'Management behaviour'. Impact is very much evident in all the other fifteen dimensions identified for the study.

Table 4.41 : Influence of the Total Family Income of the Respondents on Perception

There is no significant difference in the respondents perception of the various dimensions of organisational climate with reference to total family income.

Sl. No.	Dimensions of Organisational Climate	'H' Value	'P' Value	Result
1.	Goal clarity and acceptance	13.727	0.003	S
2.	Working conditions	54.305	0.000	S
3.	Recognition and satisfaction	43.071	0.000	S
4.	Work group co-operation, friendliness and warmth.	17.237	0.001	S
5.	Job importance, challenge and variety	31.036	0.000	S
6.	Participation and communication	30.989	0.000	S
7.	Rules and policies	108.787	0.000	S
8.	Employee commitment	69.400	0.000	S
9.	Conflict and pressure	38.578	0.000	S
10.	Fairness	65.250	0.000	S
11.	Opportunity for growth, innovation and change	14.615	0.002	S
12.	Social values and beliefs	28.860	0.000	S
13.	Professional and organisational esprit	146.271	0.000	S
14.	Management behaviour	14.070	0.003	S
15.	Events and celebrations	70.860	0.000	S
16.	Non-work related factors	64.855	0.000	S
	Overall Score	**72.753**	**0.000**	**S**

S = Significant NS = Not Significant

The data available further shows that the calculated value of the chi-square is higher than the table value (5.99) at 5 per cent level of significance. Hence the null hypothesis that there is no significant difference in the respondents' perception of the various dimensions of organisational climate with reference to the number of earning members in the family is rejected.

Table 4.41 shows that the total family income of the respondents has a significant role in influencing their perception. It also reveals that there is an absolute influence of the total family income of the respondents in their perception.

The information available also shows that the calculated value of the chi-square is higher than the table value (7.81) at 5 per cent level of significance and hence the null hypothesis is rejected. The rejection of the hypothesis enables the researcher to conclude that the total family income of the respondents has a significant role to play in influencing their perceptions of the various dimensions of organisational Climate.

Summary

Analysis of perception of respondents towards the various dimensions of organisational climate and identification of relationship between perception and socio-economic factors are the two major issues dealt with in this chapter. In order to measure the internal consistency and reliability of the items in a scale, the researcher has conducted Cronbach's Alpha test of reliability in this chapter. It also presents the socio-economic profile of the respondents and a profile of the dimensions of organisational climate. Kruscal-Wallis One-way Anova was also used in this chapter to test whether the socio-economic variables influence the perception of the respondents.

5

CHAPTER

Influence of Organisational Climate

Introduction

Human behaviour is an outcome of individual and situational factors. The role of individual factors though accepted predominant and the impact of situational factors in shaping human behaviour cannot be just ignored. More specifically the two important aspects which decide the quality of performance of an individual in a job are his perception of the various dimensions of organisational climate and his understanding or knowledge of the basic job requisites needed and possessed. An attempt has been taken in this segment of the study to find out the influence of organisational climate on the motivation and the performance of respondents. This chapter also analyses the relationship between the perception and the understanding of the basic job requisites possessed by the employees.

Climate and Motivation and Performance

The motivation and the performance of an employee in a job is determined by a number of individual and organisational factors. One such factor that contributes significantly towards individual motivation and performance in a job is organisational climate. The researchers in this portion of the study have used Lickert's five-point scaling technique to find out the influence of organisational climate on motivation and performance of respondents. A list of fifteen positive statements has been identified and included and the respondents were asked to make their opinions on the scale consisting of the items : Strongly Agree (SA), Agree (A), Undecided (UD), Disagree (DA) and Strongly Disagree (SDA). The scale items carry the scores 5, 4, 3, 2 and 1 respectively. The total score for each statement was calculated by multiplying the number of respondents in a scale with its respective score. The total score secured by each statement shows its significance in relation to other statements included in the table. The statements included, the total score secured by each statement and the grand total scores of all the statements have been shown in Table 5.1. The core aspect covered in the statements included in the questionnaire has been denoted as focus of statement in the table.

Table 5.1 and Fig. 5.1 show that the respondents complete their work everyday without any balance due to the supportive work environment and the statement carries a perception score of 847. The statement that respondents feel like coming to work every day because they find it interesting to meet their fellow employees and work happily carries a perception score of 593. The perception of respondents that the work is done sincerely because they are trusted and supported carries a score of 651 whereas the statement that the respondents prefer to take up new assignments because of the conducive work atmosphere carries the perception score of 445.

The understanding of the respondents that they are filled with enthusiasm and optimism in work because things and people around them are supportive carries a perception score of 698 and a perception score of 964 for the statement that the prevailing work atmosphere encourages to maintain team spirit in the Corporation.

Table 5.1 : Influence of Organisational Climate on Motivation and Performance

Sl. No.	Focus of Statements to find out the influence of organisational climate on motivation and performance	Types of Response and score					Total Score
		SDA	DA	UD	A	SA	
1	2	3	4	5	6	7	8
1.	The work is completed everyday without any balance because the work environment is supportive.	13	274	219	176	165	847
2.	Feel like coming to work everyday be cause it is interesting to meet people and work happily.	90	298	129	56	20	593
3.	The work is done sincerely because employees are trusted and supported positively.	31	456	39	60	65	651
4.	Prefer to take up new assignments because the work atmosphere is encouraging.	206	114	84	16	25	445
5.	Enthusiasm and optimism are found in work because things and people around are always supportive.	45	298	222	108	25	698

Table 5.1-(Contd.)

1	2	3	4	5	6	7	8
6.	The prevailing work climate encourages maintaining team spirit in the place of work.	5	238	129	292	300	964
7.	Employees are praised by their colleagues and superiors whenever they exceed the normal standard of performance.	60	124	174	228	315	901
8.	People in the work place have never dwelled on our weaknesses.	15	176	231	408	90	920
9.	Superior suggests the ways of improving the performance during the review period and they are considered positively.	5	266	219	296	75	861
10.	Employees are helped appropriately to recover from the setbacks in performance because there is good human relations in the place of work.	134	236	15	116	70	571
11.	Employees have certain goals before them to motivate themselves which are adequately supported by the work environment.	62	292	222	56	20	652

12.	The climate in the Corporation has provided the employees an emotional stability.	90	266	129	116	25	626
13.	Mutual goal setting which motivates the performance of the employees is a symbol of positive work atmosphere in the Corporation.	105	236	171	20	75	607
14.	Superior stimulates analysis of performance and setting of work objectives, which is an evidence of healthy corporate climate.	75	296	129	120	20	640
15.	The place of our work has helped us to acquire a sensible and worthwhile philosophy of life.	73	270	129	176	25	673
	Total	**1009**	**3840**	**2241**	**2244**	**1315**	**10649**

Source : Primary Data.

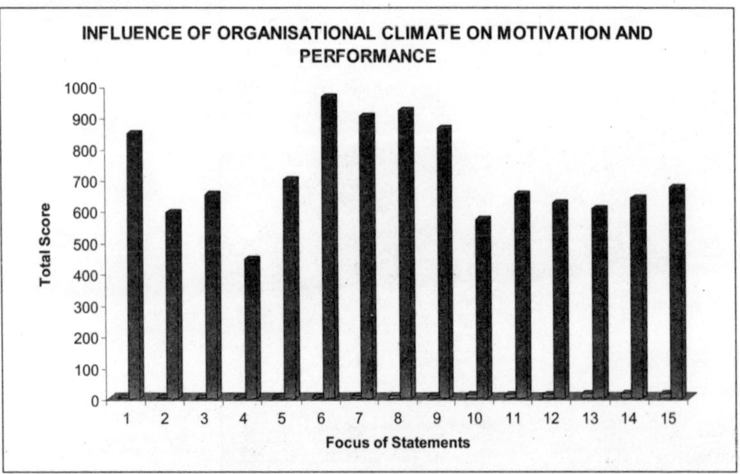

Fig. 5.1. Influence of Organisational Climate Motivation and Performance

The respondents' perception of the statement that they are praised by their colleagues and superiors when they exceed the normal standard of performance carries a score of 901 whereas the statement that their fellow employees have never dwelled on their weaknesses has a perception score of 920.

Table 5.1 also shows that the respondents view the suggestions given by their superiors positively and the statement has a perception score of 861 whereas the statement that the respondents are helped appropriately to recover from the setbacks in performance by the good human relationship prevalent in the place of work has a score of 571. The perception statement that the work goals of the respondents are duly supported by the environment carries a score of 652 and the statement that the work climate in the Corporation has provided the respondents an emotional stability has a perception score of 626.

The table further shows that mutual goal setting that takes place in the Corporation is a symbol of a positive work atmosphere and the statement has a perception score of 607 whereas the statement that the superiors encourage the respondents to analyse their work performances which is an evidence of a healthy corporate climate carries a perception score of 640. The place of work has helped the respondents to acquire a sensible and worthwhile philosophy of life and the statement carries a perception score of 673. It can also be observed that the overall score of all the statements is 10,649.

Level of Perception of Climate and Motivation and Performance

The classification of responses given by the respondents on the basis of some criteria is generally done to find out the opinion of the majority of respondents over a particular issue. Such an initiative will also enable to arrive at a meaningful conclusion.

Table 5.2 shows the classification of respondents' perception of the various statements included to find out the influence of organisational climate on motivation and performance. The perception of the respondents has been classified into three levels viz., high, moderate and low. It has been taken for the present study that, if the overall score of a respondent for each statement exceeds 70% he will be considered as having a high influence of organisational climate on motivation and performance. On the other hand a respondent will be viewed as having a low influence of organisational climate on motivation and performance if the overall score for each statement falls below 50%.

If the overall score obtained by a respondent for each statement falls between 50% and 70%, it will be viewed as an indicator of a moderate influence of organisational climate on motivation and performance.

Table 5.2 shows that the respondents complete their work without any balance due to the supportive work environment and the same has 147 (49%) respondents with low, 78 (26%) respondents with moderate and 75 (25%) respondents with high levels of perception. The perception

Table 5.2 : Level of Perception of the Influence of Organisational Climate on Motivationand Performance

Sl. No.	Focus of Statements to find out the influence of organisational climate on motivation and performance	Types of Response and score							Total Score
		SDA	DA	UD	A	SA			
1	2	3	4	5	6	7	8	9	10
1.	The work is completed everyday without any balance because the work environment is supportive.	147	49	78	26	75	25	300	100
2.	Feel like coming to work everyday because it is interesting to meet people and work happily	238	79.3	45	15	17	5.7	300	100
3.	The work is done sincerely because employees are trusted and supported positively	255	85	13	4.3	32	10.7	300	100
4.	Prefer to take up new assignments because the work atmosphere is encouraging.	266	88.7	29	9.7	5	1.6	300	100
5.	Enthusiasm and optimism are found in work because things and people around are always supportive.	195	65	75	25	30	10	300	100
6.	The prevailing work climate encourages to maintain team spirit in the place of work	117	39	47	15.7	136	45.3	300	100

7.	Employees are praised by their colleagues and superiors whenever they exceed the normal standard of performance	120	40	61	20.3	119	39.7	300	100
8.	People in the work place have never dwelled on our weaknesses.	103	34.3	77	25.7	120	40	300	100
9.	Superior suggests the ways of improving the performance during the review period and they are considered positively	135	45	75	25	90	30	300	100
10.	Employees are helped appropriately to recover from the setbacks in performance because there is good human relationship in the place of work	251	83.7	5	1.7	44	14.6	300	100
11.	Employees have certain goals before them to motivate themselves which are adequately supported by the work environment	210	70	74	24.7	16	5.3	300	100
12.	The climate within the Corporation provides the employees with emotional stability.	222	74	45	15	33	11	300	100
13.	Mutual goal setting which motivates the performance of the employees is a symbol of positive work atmosphere in the Corporation	225	75	58	19.3	17	5.7	300	100

(Contd.)

Table 5.2–(Contd.)

1	2	3	4	5	6	7	8	9	10
14.	Superior stimulates analysis of performance and setting of work objectives, which is an evidence of a healthy corporate climate	221	73.7	49	16.3	30	10	300	100
15.	The place of our work has helped us to acquire a sensible and worthwhile philosophy of life	206	68.6	47	15.7	47	15.7	300	100

Source : Primary Data.

statement that the respondents feel like coming to work everyday because of their interest in meeting their fellow employees and to work happily has 238 (79.3%) respondents with low, 45 (15%) respondents with moderate and 17 (5.7%) respondents with high levels of perception. 255 (85%) respondents have low, 13 (4.3%) respondents have moderate and 32 (10.7%) respondents have high perception levels regarding the statement that their work is done sincerely due to the trust and the support extended to them. The perception statement that the respondents prefer to take up new assignments because of the encouraging work climate prevalent in the Corporation has 266 (88.7%) respondents with low, 29 (9.7%) respondents with moderate and 5 (1.6%) respondents with high levels of perception. 195 (65%) respondents with low, 75 (25%) respondents with moderate and 30 (10%) respondents with high perception levels have been identified for the statement that the respondents are filled with enthusiasm and optimism because they find that the people and things around them are supportive.

The perception statement that the prevailing work climate encourages the respondents to maintain team spirit in the Corporation has 117 (39%) respondents with low, 47 (15.7%) respondents with moderate and 136 (45.3%) respondents with high perception levels. 120 (40%) respondents with low, 61 (20.3%) respondents with moderate and 119 (39.7%) respondents with high levels of perception have been identified for the perception statement that they are praised by their colleagues and superiors when they exceed the normal standard of performance. The statement that the work atmosphere never allows the fellow employees to dwell on their weaknesses has 103 (34.3%) respondents with low, 77 (25.7%) respondents with moderate and 120 (40%) respondents with high levels of perception. 135 (45%) respondents with low, 75 (25%) respondents with moderate and 90 (30%) respondents with high levels of perception have been identified for the perception statement that their superiors suggest the ways of improving the performance and the same have been viewed positively. The perception statement that the respondents are helped appropriately to recover from the setbacks in performance because there is good human relationship in the place of work has 251 (83.7%) respondents with low, 5 (1.7%) respondents with moderate and 44 (14.6%) respondents with high levels of perception.

It could further be observed from the given table that the perception statement on the availability of goals before the respondents to motivate their performance has 210 (70%) respondents with low, 74 (24.7%) respondents with moderate and 16 (5.3%) respondents with high levels of perception. 222 (74%) respondents with low, 45 (15%) respondents with moderate and 33 (11%) respondents with high levels of perception have been found for the statement that the prevailing climate in the Corporation provides them with emotional stability. Considering mutual goal setting as a symbol of the prevalent positive work atmosphere has 225 (75%) respondents with low, 58 (19.3%) respondents with moderate and the remaining 17 (5.7%) respondents with high perception levels. 221 (73.7%) respondents with low, 49 (16.3.%) respondents with moderate and 30 (10%) respondents with high perception levels have been found for the statement that the superiors encourage the respondents to analyse their work performance and set their own work objectives, which is an evidence of a healthy organisational climate. The classification further shows that the perception statement that the work place is considered a source of acquiring a sensible and worthwhile philosophy of life has 206 (68.6%) respondents with low, 47 (15.7%) with moderate and the remaining 47 (15.7%) respondents with high levels of perception.

Relationship between Climate and Motivation and Performance

Motivating employees towards successful performance in a job is becoming a tough task and employers need to adopt a dynamic approach in motivation and dealing with issues related to task accomplishment. Human performance is a product of a number of aspects present in individuals and the organisation. The role of a conducive environment prevailing around the place of work is of paramount importance since it adds strength to effective human performance in a work setting. The researcher in this small segment of the study has taken an attempt to find out the correlation between the various dimensions of organisational climate and motivation and performance of the respondents in the job.

Table 5.3 shows that there is low correlation (0.4594) between the dimension 'Goal clarity and acceptance' and 'Motivation and performance'. It can be further noted from the table that there is negative correlation (-0.0072) between the organisational climate dimension 'Working conditions' and 'Motivation and performance'.

The correlation between the dimension 'Recognition and satisfaction' and 'Motivation and performance' is low (0.2217). There is high correlation (0.5560) between 'Motivation and performance' and the organisational climate dimension, 'Work group co-operation, friendliness and warmth'.

It can also be noted that there is low correlation (0.3391) between the organisational climate dimension 'Job importance, challenge and variety' and 'Motivation and performance'. There is low correlation (0.2766) between 'Motivation and performance' and the organisational climate dimension 'Participation and communication'.

The degree of correlation is found to be low (0.0978) between the dimension 'Rules and policies' and 'Motivation and performance'. Low correlation (0.2437) is also found between 'Motivation and performance' and the climate dimension 'Employee commitment'.

The table also shows that there is negative correlation (-0.0156) between the organisational climate dimension 'Conflict and pressure' and 'Motivation and performance'.

Table 5.3 : Correlation between the Dimensions of Organisational Climate and Motivation and Performance

Sl. No.	Dimensions of Organisational Climate	$r(X,Y)$	r^2	t	p
1.	Goal clarity and acceptance	0.4594	0.2110	8.9276	0.0000
2.	Working conditions	-0.0072	0.0001	-0.1247	0.9009
3.	Recognition and satisfaction	0.2217	0.0492	3.9253	0.0001
4.	Workgroup co-operation, friendliness and warmth	0.5560	0.3091	11.5461	0.0000
5.	Job importance, challenge and variety	0.3391	0.1150	6.2231	0.0000
6.	Participation and communication	0.2766	0.0765	4.9690	0.0000
7.	Rules and policies	0.0978	0.0096	1.6962	0.0909
8.	Employee commitment	0.2437	0.0594	4.3374	0.0000
9.	Conflict and pressure	-0.0156	0.0002	-0.2687	0.7884
10.	Fairness	0.1618	0.0262	2.8297	0.0050
11.	Opportunity for growth, innovation and change	0.2633	0.0693	4.7113	0.0000
12.	Social values and beliefs	0.1482	0.0220	2.5864	0.0102
13.	Professional and organisational esprit	0.0849	0.0072	1.4712	0.1423
14.	Management behaviour	-0.4059	0.1647	-7.6662	0.0000
15.	Events and celebrations	0.4267	0.1821	8.1445	0.0000
16.	Non-work related factors	0.2637	0.0695	4.7192	0.0000

Source : Primary Data. Significant at 5% level

There is low correlation (0.1618) between 'Motivation and performance' and the organisational climate dimension 'Fairness'.

Low correlation (0.2633) is again found between the dimension 'Opportunity for growth, innovation and change' and 'Motivation and performance'. It can be further noted that the correlation (0.1482) between 'Motivation and performance' and the climate dimension 'Social values and belief' is also low.

The degree of correlation (0.0849) between the dimension 'Professional and organisational esprit' and 'Motivation and performance' is found to be low. The table also reveals that there is negative correlation (-0.4059) between 'Motivation and performance' and the organisational climate dimension 'Management behaviour'.

The correlation (0.4267) between the dimension 'Events and celebrations' and 'Motivation and performance' is also found to be low. There is low correlation (0.2637) between 'Motivation and performance' and the organisational climate dimension 'Non-work related factors'.

Perception of Basic Job Requisites

The overall performance of employees in a job depends on a number of internal and external factors. External factors are those which are present around the job in which the individual employee has less control. Contrarily, internal factors are those in which the individual employee has higher control over the same. The employees who understand their possession of the basic job requisites enlarges his vision towards performance and people. More specifically, the strength of job knowledge that one has influences his overall perception towards job and hence an effort has been taken to find out the respondents' perception of the possession of basic job requisites and the same has been presented in Table 5.4 and Fig. 5.2.

Table 5.4 : Respondents' Perception of the Possession of Basic Job Requisites

Sl. No.	Focus of Statements to find out the influence of organisational climate on motivation and performance	Types of Response and score					Total Score
		SDA	DA	UD	A	SA	
1	2	3	4	5	6	7	8
1.	Believed that the required knowledge to do the job is possessed	5	54	174	596	305	1134
2.	The performance in the job can be quantified against the standards set already	4	148	171	304	445	1072
3.	The job is completed well in time	14	178	273	352	90	907
4.	Cost effectiveness is ensured in the work	15	270	312	124	75	796
5.	Satisfactory level of performance is maintained in the job	28	34	135	536	380	1113
6.	There are specific achievements in the job	60	302	87	124	145	718
7.	Thoroughness and accuracy are ensured in the job	74	152	303	16	225	770
8.	Expected rate of progress is present in the job	30	206	231	300	75	842
9.	Regularity, punctuality and attentiveness are maintained in the job	45	86	231	420	150	932

10.	Real interest is maintained in the job entrusted	90	234	81	244	25	674
11.	The first priority in the work place is to do the job	45	148	312	180	160	845
12.	Ready to increase the efficiency in the job	116	322	42	20	20	520
13.	Ready to accept more difficult than simple jobs	90	294	84	20	150	638
14.	Job decisions at the employees' level are taken after careful consideration	14	178	174	540	20	926
15.	Job decisions are implemented appropriately without any deviation	4	88	177	416	445	1130
	Total	**634**	**2694**	**2787**	**2710**	**4192**	**13,017**

Source : Primary Data.

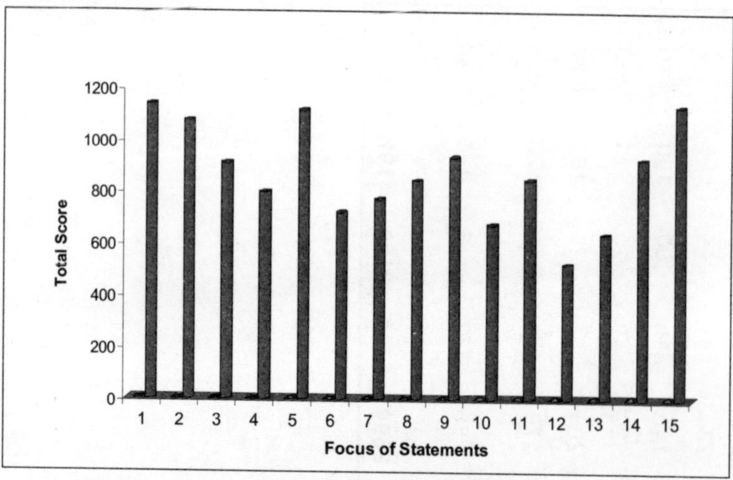

Fig. 5.2 : Respondents' Perception of the Possession of basic Job Requisites

Table 5.4 shows the scores obtained by each statement included to find out the respondents' perception of the possession of certain basic job requisites. A score of 1134 has been obtained by the statement that the respondents possess the required knowledge to do the job. The statement that the performance of respondents can be quantified against the standards set already carries a score of 1072. The table also shows that the perception of respondents that the job is completed well in time carries a score of 907.

The perception statement that cost effectiveness is ensured in the work carries a score of 796 and the statement that satisfactory level of performance is maintained in the job carries a score of 1113. A perception score of 718 has been obtained for the statement that there are specific achievements in the job of the respondents.

A perception score 770 has been obtained by the statement that thoroughness and accuracy are ensured by the respondents in their job. The statement that the expected rate of progress is present in the job carries a score of 842. The statement that regularity, punctuality and attentiveness are maintained in the job performed by the respondents carries a score of 932.

The table given above also shows that real interest is maintained in the job entrusted to the respondents and it carries a perception score of 674. The statement that the first priority of the respondents in the work place is to do the job carries a score of 845. The statement that the respondents are ready to increase their efficiency in the job has a score of 520.

The table further shows that the statement on the readiness of the respondents to accept more difficult than simple job carries a score of 638. A score of 926 has been obtained by the statement that the job decisions at the level of the respondents are taken after careful consideration. The statement that the job decisions are implemented appropriately without any deviation has a score of 1130. It can also be observed that the overall score of all the statements included in Table 5.2 is 13,017.

Level of Perception of Basic Job Requisites

Knowing the opinion of respondents on a particular issue and classifying them on the basis of certain criteria enables one to understand the composite opinion of the respondents. Collection and analysis of the level of the perception of employees on issues pertaining to a job helps one to know the strength and the weaknesses in a job. Analysing the perception of the possession of basic job requisites is considered important as it has an influence of climate dimensions. Hence the level of the respondents' perception of the possession of basic job requisites are collected and presented in Table 5.5.

It is clear from Table 5.5 that the perception statement revealing the belief of the respondents that they possess the required knowledge to do the job has 33 (11%) respondents with low, 58 (19.3%) respondents with moderate and 209

Table 5.5 : Level of the Respondents' Perception of the Possession of Basic Job Requisites

Sl. No.	Focus of statements to find out the perception of the possession of 'Basic job requisites'	Level of perception						Total	
		Low		Moderate		High			
		No. of Respon-dents	%	No. of Respon-dents	%	No. of Respon-dents	%	No. of Respon-dents	%
1	2	3	4	5	6	7	8	9	10
1.	Believe that the required knowledge to do the job is possessed	33	11	58	19.3	209	69.7	300	100
2.	The performance in the job can be quantified against the standards set already	75	25	62	20.7	163	54.3	300	100
3.	The job is completed well in time	101	33.7	92	30.7	107	35.6	300	100
4.	Cost effectiveness is ensured in the work	148	49.3	104	34.7	48	16	300	100

5.	Satisfactory level of performance is maintained in the job	41	13.6	45	15	214	71.4	300	100
6.	There are specific achievements in my job	213	71	27	9	60	20	300	100
7.	Thoroughness and accuracy are ensured in the job	154	51.3	103	34.3	43	14.4	300	100
8.	Expected rate of progress is present in the job	133	44.3	73	24.3	94	31.4	300	100
9.	Regularity, punctuality and attentiveness are maintained in the job	93	31	71	23.7	136	45.3	300	100
10.	Real interest is maintained in the job entrusted	214	71.3	30	10	56	18.7	300	100
11.	The first priority in the place of work is to do my job	122	40.7	106	35.3	72	24	300	100
12.	Ready to increase the efficiency in the job	283	94.3	13	4.3	4	1.4	300	100
13.	Ready to accept more difficult than simple jobs	240	80	28	9.3	32	10.7	300	100

(Contd.)

Tabnle 5.5–(Contd.)

1	2	3	4	5	6	7	8	9	10
14.	Job decisions at the employees' level are taken after careful consideration.	106	35.3	59	19.7	135	45	300	100
15.	Job decisions are followed appropriately without any deviation	48	16	56	18.7	196	65.3	300	100

Source : Primary Data

(69.7%) respondents with high levels of perception. The statement that the performance of the respondents in the job can be quantified against the standards set already has 75 (25%) respondents with low, 62 (20.7%) respondents with moderate and 163 (54.3%) respondents with high levels of perception. 101 (33.7%) respondents with low, 92 (30.7%) respondents with moderate and 107 (35.6%) respondents with high levels of perception have been found out for the statement that the job is completed well in time.

The statement on cost effectiveness has 148 (49.3%) respondents with low, 104 (34.7%) respondents with moderate and the remaining 48 (16%) respondents with high levels of perception. Forty-one (13.6%) respondents with low, 45 (15%) respondents with moderate and 214 (71.4%) respondents with high levels of perception have been identified for the statement that satisfactory level of performance has been maintained by the respondents in their job. The statement that the respondents have specific achievements in their job has 213 (71%), 27 (9%) and 60 (20%) respondents with low, moderate and high levels of perception respectively.

The table also shows that the statement on thoroughness and accuracy in job has 154 (51.3%) respondents with low level of perception, 103 (34.3%) respondents with moderate level of perception and 43 (14.4%) respondents with high level of perception. 133 (44.3%) respondents with low, 73 (24.3%) respondents with moderate and the remaining 94 (31.4%) respondents with high levels of perception have been identified for the statement that the respondents found the expected rate of progress in their job. The statement on regularity, punctuality and attentiveness in the job has 93 (31%) respondents with low level of perception, 71 (23.7%) respondents with moderate level of perception and 136 (45.3%) respondents with high level of perception.

It could also be noted that the statement regarding the real interest of the respondents in the job entrusted to them has 214 (71.3%), 30 (10%) and 56 (18.7%) respondents with low, moderate and high levels of perception respectively.

The statement on the priority of the respondents in the work place has 122 (40.7%) respondents with low level of perception, 106 (35.3%) respondents with moderate level of perception and 72 (24%) respondents with high level of perception. 283 (94.3%) respondents with low, 13 (4.3%) respondents with moderate and 4 (1.4%) of the respondents with high level of perception have been identified for the statement that the respondents are ready to increase their efficiency in the job.

A total of 240 (80%) respondents with low, 28 (9.3%) respondents with moderate and 32 (10.7%) respondents with high levels of perception have been identified for the perception statement that the respondents are ready to accept more difficult than simple jobs. Table 5.5 further shows that the perception statement depicting the decision making done at the level of respondents after careful consideration has 106 (35.3%), 59 (19.7%) and 135 (45%) respondents with low, moderate and high levels of perception respectively. The statement on adherence to job decisions by the respondents without any deviation has 48 (16%), 56 (18.7%) and 196 (65.3%) respondents with low, medium and high levels of perception respectively.

Relationship between Climate and Basic Job Requisites

Finding the correlation between any two factors brings out the nature of relationship among them. Such an attempt is vital as it helps to take decisions concretely on different factors pertaining to an issue. The researcher in this small segment of the study has taken an attempt to find out the correlation between the dimensions of organisational climate and the possession of basic job requisites.

Table 5.6 clearly shows that there is low correlation (0.3055) between the dimension 'Goal clarity, acceptance' and the 'Basic job requisites' score available for the respondents. Low correlation (0.3324) is found between

Table 5.6 : Correlation between the Dimensions of Organisational Climate and the Possession of basic Job Requisites

Sl.No.	Dimensions of Organisational Climate	$r(X,Y)$	r^2	t	p
1.	Goal clarity, acceptance	0.3055	0.0933	5.5382	0.0000
2.	Working conditions	0.3324	0.1105	-6.0833	0.0000
3.	Recognition and satisfaction	0.2431	0.0591	4.3259	0.0000
4.	Workgroup co-operation, friendliness and warmth	0.5991	0.3589	12.9160	0.0000
5.	Job importance, challenge and variety	0.4872	0.2374	9.6308	0.0000
6.	Participation and communication	0.1476	0.0218	2.5767	0.0105
7.	Rules and policies	-0.1334	0.0178	-2.3232	0.0208
8.	Employee commitment	0.2090	0.0437	3.6890	0.0003
9.	Conflict and pressure	-0.2454	0.0602	-4.3704	0.0000
10.	Fairness	-0.2516	0.0633	-4.4869	0.0000
11.	Opportunity for growth, innovation and change	0.5484	0.3007	11.3208	0.0000
12.	Social values and beliefs	0.4825	0.2328	9.5103	0.0000
13.	Professional and organisational esprit	0.3482	0.1213	6.4129	0.0000
14.	Management behaviour	0.0950	0.0090	1.6482	0.1004
15.	Events and celebrations	0.4238	0.1796	8.0770	0.0000
16.	Non-work related factors	0.0357	0.0013	0.6167	0.5379

Source : Primary Data

Significant at 5% level

the organisational climate dimension 'Working conditions' and the available score for 'Basic job requisites' possessed by the respondents. The table further shows that there is low correlation (0.2431) between the dimension 'Recognition and satisfaction' and the score available for the possession of certain 'Basic job requisites' by the respondents.

It can also be learnt from the table that there is high correlation (0.5991) between the organisational climate dimension 'Work group co-operation, friendliness and warmth' and the perception score of the respondents in possessing the 'Basic job requisites'. Low correlation (0.4872) has been found between the organisational climate dimension 'Job importance, challenge and variety' and the available score for 'Basic job requisites' possessed by the respondents. Low correlation is also found (0.1476) between the dimension 'Participation and communication' and the 'Basic job requisites' score obtained by the respondents.

As it has been shown in Table 5.6, negative correlation (-0.1334) has been identified between the organisational climate dimension 'Rules and policies' and the available score for the 'Basic job requisites' possessed by the respondents. Low correlation (0.2090) has also been found between the dimension 'Employee commitment' and the score available for the possession of certain 'Basic job requisites' by the respondents. Negative correlation (-0.2454) has been identified between the organisational climate dimension 'Conflict and pressure' and the available score for the 'Basic job requisites' possessed by the respondents.

Table 5.6 further shows that there is negative correlation (-0.2516) between the dimension 'Fairness' and the 'Basic job requisites' score obtained by the respondents. The dimension 'Opportunity for growth, innovation and change' has high correlation (0.5484) with the available score for 'Basic job requisites' possessed by the respondents. There is a low correlation (0.4825) between the dimension 'Social values and beliefs' and the 'Basic job requisites' score obtained by the respondents.

Low correlation (0.3482) has been found out between the dimension 'Professional and organisational esprit' and the 'Basic job requisites' score available for the respondents. It has been further noted that there is low correlation (0.9050) between the organisational climate dimension 'Management behaviour' and the 'Basic job requisites' score obtained by the respondents. There is a low correlation (0.4238) between the dimension 'Events and celebrations' and the available score for 'Basic job requisites' possessed by the respondents. The table also shows that there is low correlation (0.0357) between the organisational climate dimension 'Non-work related factors' and the 'Basic job requisites' score available for the respondents.

Summary

This chapter finds out the influence of organisational climate on motivation and performance. The influence of the climate has been further classified into low, moderate and high levels for further analysis. An initiative has also been taken to find out the correlation between the dimensions of organisational climate and motivation and performance. The chapter also reveals the respondents' perception of the possession of basic job requisites along with the classification of the same into three levels. This chapter further shows the correlation between the dimensions of organisational climate and the possession of basic job requisites by the respondents.

6

CHAPTER

Preference Over the Different Aspects of Work Life

Introduction

Climate is a composite perception of its stakeholder, especially by the employees, of the various aspects of work in an organisation. An assessment of composite perception always enables the people concerned to understand the strengths and weaknesses in the system as perceived by its own work force. Such an attempt can also enable the management of the organisation to weigh again the tasks, processes and the end results achieved. Any organisation which aims at scaling better heights in its performance is supposed to possess a right attitude towards the feeling of its employees. Reasonable care extended to the feelings of the workers concerning the various aspects of worklife will ensure a sense of satisfaction in the individual worker and such satisfaction will definitely be witnessed in the form of involvement, perfection, co-operation etc., in work.

An attempt has been made in this section of the study to present the ranks given by the respondents according to their preference for the different aspects affecting organisational climate in the study area. Each respondent was asked to identify any five important aspects according to their preference that are standing as stumbling blocks for the creation of a conducive organisational climate. The various aspects identified as affecting organisational climate in the study area are as follows :

1. Non-availability of health care facilities
2. Poor working conditions of buses
3. Lengthy legal formalities in case of accidents
4. Targeted route collection
5. Lack of pension schemes for employees
6. Attachment of buses by courts for accident claims
7. Coverage of targeted kilometres per litre of diesel
8. Suspension of employees for accidents
9. Increased work load
10. Lack of co-operation from the general public
11. Cancellation of driving license for accidents
12. Absense of increase in salary in tune with experience
13. Poor family income due to cancellation of driving licence
14. Vast difference in pay among the employees
15. Lack of motivation by the administration
16. Routes with poor collection.

The aspects ranked by the respondents were analysed on the basis of socio-economic variables of the respondents such as Age, Marital status, Number of Dependents, Experience etc.

Ranking of Different Aspects Affecting Organisational Climate

The first step involved in the process of ranking the different aspects affecting organisational climate is arriving at the weighted scores. The required weighted scores have been calculated on the basis of the ranks given to them by the respondents.

For arriving at the weighted score, the aspect that was identified as the first and the foremost one as affecting the organisational climate carried five points. The aspects ranked second, third, fourth and fifth have carried four, three, two and one points respectively. Therefore the weighted score for each of the aspects is the product of the number of respondents who have given first, second, third, fourth and fifth ranks and the corresponding points: five, four, three, two and one respectively. The scores obtained by each aspect are added to obtain the weighted score.

Table 6.1 and Fig. 6.1 describe the various aspects identified as affecting organisational climate, the weighted scores and the ranks obtained by each of them. Spearman's rank order correlation and 't' test are also used to find out the composite relationship among the different groups with varied socio-economic background in viewing the different aspects affecting organisational climate.

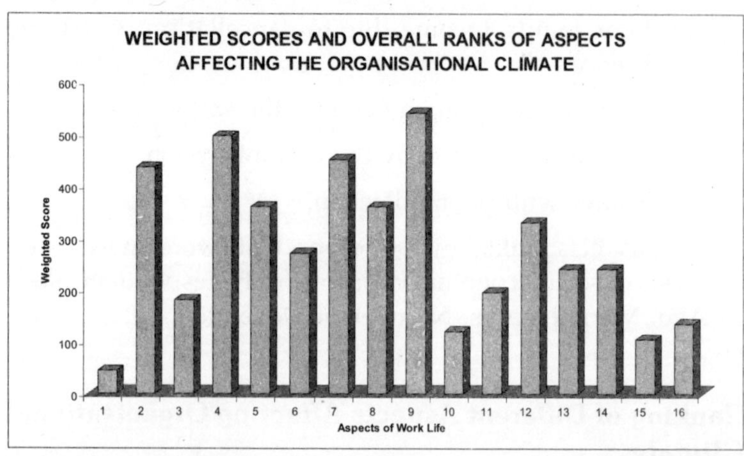

Fig. 6.1. Weighted Scores and Overall Ranks of Aspects Afecting the Organisational Climate

Table 6.1 shows that the aspect 'Increased workload' has been viewed as the prime aspect that affects the climate in the organisation, followed by the aspect 'Targeted route collection' with the second rank. The third overall position has been obtained by the aspect 'Coverage of targeted kilometres per litre of diesel' as affecting the prevailing organisational climate. 'Poor working conditions of buses' has been viewed as the fourth major aspect that creates an impact in the climate of the organisation. The overall fifth rank has been given to the elements 'Lack of pension schemes for employees' and 'Suspension of employees for accidents.' It can also be seen that the least rank was given to the aspect 'Non-availability of health care facilities' by the respondents, preceded by the element 'Lack of motivation by the administration' as the second least element affecting the climate in the organisation.' The elements 'Lack of co-operation from the general public' and 'Routes with poor collection' have been identified as the third and fourth least factors affecting the climate in the organisation. The element 'Lengthy legal formalities in case of accidents' ranks fifth least among the various aspects affecting the prevailing work climate in the organisation.

Table 6.2 shows that the respondents who are below 30 years of age have identified 'Vast difference in pay among the employees' as the most important element affecting organisational climate, followed by 'Coverage of targeted kilometers per litre of diesel' as the second important aspect that affects the prevailing organisational climate. The least important rank is given to aspects other than those of

'Non-availability of health care facilities', 'Lack of pension schemes for employees', 'Attachment of buses by courts for accident claims', 'Increased work load' and 'Absence of increase in salary in tune with experience'. The respondents of 31-40 years age group have identified 'Increased work load' as the prime aspect and 'Coverage of targeted kilometers per litre of diesel' as the second important aspect that bears an

Table 6.1 : Weighted Score and Overall Ranks of Aspects Affecting the Organisational Climate

Sl. No	Aspects of Work Life	Number of respondents opted					Weighted Score	Overall Rank
		Rank 1	Rank 2	Rank 3	Rank 4	Rank 5		
1	2	3	4	5	6	7	8	9
1.	Non-availability of health care facilities	0	0	0	15	15	45	16
2.	Poor working conditions of buses	15	45	45	0	45	435	4
3.	Lengthy legal formalities in case of accidents	15	0	15	15	30	180	12
4.	Targeted route collection	60	0	30	45	15	495	2
5.	Lack of pension schemes for employees	15	60	0	15	15	360	5
6.	Attachment of buses by courts for accident claims	15	0	45	30	0	270	8
7.	Coverage of targeted kilometers per litre of diesel	45	30	15	15	30	450	3
8.	Suspension of employees for accidents	15	45	15	30	0	360	5
9.	Increased work load	45	30	45	30	0	540	1
10.	Lack of co-operation from the general public	0	0	15	15	45	120	14

11.	Cancellation of driving license for accidents	0	30	15	15	0	195	11
12.	Absence of increase in salary based on experience	15	30	30	15	15	330	7
13.	Poor family income due to cancellation of driving license	15	15	0	30	45	240	9
14.	Vast difference in pay among the employees	30	0	15	15	15	240	9
15.	Lack of motivation by the administration	0	15	0	15	15	105	15
16.	Routes with poor collection	15	0	15	0	15	135	13

Source : Primary Data.

Table 6.1 : Weighted Score and Overall Ranks of Aspects Affecting the Organisational Climate

Sl. No.	Aspects of Work Life	Age (in years) & Ranks									
		Below 30	31-40	41-50	Over 50	1&2 d_1^2	1&3 d_2^2	1&4 d_3^2	1&3 d_4^2	1&4 d_5^2	1&5 d_6^2
1	2	3	4	5	6	7	8	9	10	11	12
1.	Non-availability of health care facilities	7	14	14	13	49	49	36	0	1	1
2.	Poor working conditions of buses	8	4	1	1	16	49	49	9	9	0
3.	Lengthy legal formalities in case of accidents	8	9	14	3	1	36	25	25	36	121
4.	Targeted route collection	8	3	2	4	25	36	16	1	1	4
5.	Lack of pension schemes for employees	3	7	4	5	16	1	4	9	4	1
6.	Attachment of buses by courts for accident claims	5	14	2	13	81	9	64	144	1	121
7.	Coverage of targeted kilometres per litre of diesel	2	2	9	5	0	49	9	49	9	16
8.	Suspension of employees for accidents	8	11	5	1	9	9	49	36	100	16
9.	Increased work load	3	1	5	8	4	4	25	16	49	9
10.	Lack of co-operation from the general public	8	14	9	11	36	1	9	25	9	4

11.	Cancellation of driving license for accidents	8	9	12	8	1	16	0	9	1	16
12.	Absence of increase in salary based on experience	5	4	7	8	1	4	9	9	16	1
13.	Poor family income due to cancellation of driving license	8	7	7	11	1	1	9	0	16	16
14.	Vast difference in pay among the employees	1	11	9	13	100	64	144	4	4	16
15.	Lack of motivation by the administration	8	13	14	5	25	36	9	1	64	81
16.	Routes with poor collection	8	4	13	13	16	25	25	81	81	0
	Total					Σd_1^2	Σd_2^2	Σd_3^2	Σd_4^2	Σd_5^2	Σd_6^2

Source : Primary Data.

impact on organisational climate. The least aspects identified by the respondents of this age group are 'Non-availability of health care facilities', 'Attachment of buses by courts for accident claims' and 'Lack of co-operation from the general public'. 'Poor working conditions of buses' is the first aspect identified by the respondents of age group 41- 50 years, followed by the aspects 'Targeted route collection' and 'Attachment of buses by courts for accident claims' as the aspects next responsible for the prevailing organisational climate. 'Non-availability of health care facilities', 'Lengthy legal formalities in case of accidents' and 'Lack of motivation by the administration' are the aspects identified by the respondents of this age group as of least importance.

The aspects 'Poor working conditions of buses' and 'Suspension of employees for accidents' are identified by the respondents of the age group over 50 years as the prime reason, followed by 'Lengthy legal formalities in case of accidents' as the next reason being responsible for the existing organisational climate. 'Non-availability of health care facilities', 'Attachment of buses by courts for accident claims', 'Vast difference in pay among the employees' and 'Routes with poor collection' are identified by this age group as aspects least responsible for the prevailing organisational climate.

Table 6.3 : Correlation between the Different Age Groups of Respondents

Sl. No.	Age Group for Analysis	'R' Value	't' Value	'P' Value	Result
1.	Below 30 & 31 to 40 years	0.171	0.65	0.526	NS
2.	Below 30 & 41 to 50 years	0.148	0.56	0.584	NS
3.	Below 30 & over 50 years	-0.317	-1.251	0.231	NS
4.	31 to 40 & 41 to 50 years	0.337	1.342	0.2	NS
5.	31 to 40 & over 50 years	0.351	1.404	0.18	NS
6.	41 to 50 & over 50 years	0.289	1.132	0.27	NS

Source: Primary data

Table 6.4 : Status of the Respondents and Aspects Ranked as Affecting the Organisational Climate

Sl.No.	Aspects of Work Life	Status & Ranks		
		Married	Unmarried	1 & $2d_1^2$
1.	Non-availability of health care facilities	16	12	16
2.	Poor working conditions of buses	4	2	4
3.	Lengthy legal formalities in case of accidents	9	12	9
4.	Targeted route collection	1	10	81
5.	Lack of pension schemes for employees	5	4	1
6.	Attachment of buses by courts for accident claims	7	10	9
7.	Coverage of targeted kilometers per litre of diesel	2	6	16
8.	Suspension of employees for accidents	9	1	64
9.	Increased work load	2	2	0
10.	Lack of co-operation from the general public	13	14	1
11.	Cancellation of driving license for accidents	7	14	49
12.	Absence of increase in salary in tune with experience	6	5	1
13.	Poor family income due to cancellation of driving license	12	8	16
14.	Vast difference in pay among the employees	11	6	25
15.	Lack of motivation by the administration	14	14	0
16.	Routes with poor collection	15	8	49
	Total			**Sd_1^2 341**

Source: Primary Data.

Table 6.3 shows the relationship among the different age groups in viewing the aspects affecting organisational climate. The co-efficient of correlation among the different age groups in ranking the different aspects affecting organisational climate is below 0.5 which is low. Since the 'P' value among the different age groups is greater than 0.05 at 5 per cent level of significance, the relationship among different age groups of employees is not significant.

Table 6.4 shows that the married segment of the work-force has identified 'Targeted route collection' as the prime aspect that affects the organisational climate followed by the aspects 'Coverage of targeted kilometres per litre of diesel' and 'Increased work load' as the next important aspects affecting climate in the organisation. This segment of the respondents have also recognised that 'Non-availability of health care facilities' is the least important aspect that affects the climate in the organisation. In the unmarried segment of the respondents, the first aspect identified as affecting the climate is 'Suspension of employees for accidents' followed by the elements 'Poor working conditions of buses' as the next important aspect. 'Lack of co-operation from the general public', 'Cancellation of driving license for accidents' and 'Lack of motivation by the administration' are the least preferred aspects identified by this segment of the respondents as affecting the organisational climate.

Table 6.5 shows the relationship between the two status groups in viewing the different aspects responsible for organisational climate. It is clear that the co-efficient of correlation between the two status groups in ranking the

Table 6.5 : Correlation between the Different Status Groups of Respondents

Status Groups for Analysis	'R' Value	't' Value	'P' Value	Result
Married & Unmarried	0.48220	2.05948	0.05855	NS

Source : Primary Data.

Table 6.6 : Number of Dependents in the Family of the Respondents and Aspects Ranked as Affecting the Organisational Climate

Sl. No.	Aspects of Life	Number of Dependents & Ranks					
		1 or 2	3 or 4	5 or 6	1&2 d_1^2	1&3 d_2^2	2&3 d_3^2
1	2	3	3	4	5	6	7
1.	Non-availability of health care facilities	13	16	8	9	25	64
2.	Poor working conditions of buses	3	1	5	4	4	16
3.	Lengthy legal formalities in case of accidents	13	7	5	36	64	4
4.	Targeted route collection	2	7	8	25	36	1
5.	Lack of pension schemes for employees	5	12	2	49	9	100
6.	Attachment of buses by courts for accident claims	7	2	8	25	1	36
7.	Coverage of targeted kilometres per litre of diesel	5	2	1	9	16	1
8.	Suspension of employees for accidents	4	10	8	36	16	4
9.	Increased work load	1	10	8	81	49	4
10.	Lack of co-operation from the general public	12	12	8	0	16	16

11.	Cancellation of driving license for accidents	16	5	4	121	144	1
12.	Absence of increase in salary in tune with experience	9	5	3	16	36	4
13.	Poor family income due to cancellation of license	7	7	8	0	1	1
14.	Vast difference in pay among the employees	9	2	7	49	4	25
15.	Lack of motivation by the administration	13	12	8	1	25	16
16.	Routes with poor collection	9	12	8	9	1	16
	Total				**Σd_1^2 470**	**Σd_2^2 447**	**Σd_3^2 309**

Source: Primary Data.

aspects affecting organisational climate is lower than the required value of 0.5. It could also be seen that the 'P' value is greater than the required value of 0.05 at 5 per cent level of significance. Hence, the relationship among different status groups of employees is not significant.

Table 6.6 shows that the respondents with one or two dependents in the family have identified 'Increased work load' as the vital aspect that contributes negatively towards the climate prevailing in the organisation. 'Targeted route collection' is the second major aspect affecting the climate in the organisation as identified by the same segment of the respondents. 'Cancellation of driving license for accidents' is the least aspect identified by this group of respondents as influencing the climate in the organisation. As far as the respondents who have 3 or 4 dependents are concerned, 'Poor working conditions of buses' ranked as the most important aspect followed by the elements 'Attachment of buses by courts for accident claims', 'Coverage of targeted kilometers per litre of diesel' and 'Vast difference in pay among the employees' as next responsible for the work atmosphere prevailing in the organisation. The least aspect identified by this segment of respondents as being responsible for the work climate in the organisation is 'Non availability of health care facilities'. The aspect 'Coverage of targeted kilometers per litre of diesel' has been given the first rank by the respondents who have 5 or 6 dependents followed by the aspect 'Lack of Pension schemes for employees' as the next factor responsible for the prevailing climate in the organisation. The least important rank is given to the elements other than those of 'Poor working conditions of buses', 'Lengthy legal formalities in case of accidents', 'Cancellation of driving license for accidents', 'Absence of increase in salary in tune with experience' and 'Vast difference in pay among the employees'.

Table 6.7 shows the correlation between and the nature of relationship among the different dependent groups in looking at the aspects affecting the prevailing organisational climate. It is evident from the low score of correlation co-efficient which is below 0.5 in ranking the different aspects affecting organisational climate that the groups with different strengths of dependents are not viewing the aspects affecting the climate in the organisation alike. Since the 'P' value among the different segments of respondents with a varied number of dependent groups is greater than 0.05, it can be concluded that the relationship among them in ranking the different aspects responsible for the existing climate in the organisation is not significant.

Table 6.7 : Correlation between the Different Dependent Groups of Respondents

Dependent Groups for Analysis	'R' Value	't' Value	'P' Value	Result
Below 2 & 3 or 4	0.25189	0.97388	0.34665	NS
Below 2 & 5 or 6	-0.05882	-0.22048	0.82868	NS
3 or 4 & 5 or 6	0.46427	1.96134	0.07004	NS

Source : Primary Data

Table 6.8 shows that the respondents with below 10 years of work experience have identified 'Coverage of targeted kilometers per litre of diesel' as the most important aspect that affects the climate in the organisation followed by the aspect 'Lengthy legal formalities in case of accidents' getting the second rank. The least rank assigned by this group of respondents goes to the elements 'Targeted route collection' and 'Lack of motivation by the administration'. The respondents with 11 to 20 years of experience have chosen 'Targeted route collection' as the prime factor responsible for the work climate prevailing in their organisation followed by the element 'Increased work load' getting the second rank. The least important elements identified by this segment of

Table 6.8 : Work Experience of the Respondents and Aspects Ranked as Affecting the Climate in the Organisation

Sl. No.	Aspects of Work Life	Work Experience & Ranks				1&2 d_1^2	1&3 d_2^2	1&4 d_3^2	1&3 d_4^2	1&4 d_5^2	1&5 d_6^2
		Below 10 yrs	31-20 yrs	21-30 yrs	Over 30 yrs						
1	2	3	4	5	6	7	8	9	10	11	12
1.	Non-availability of health care facilities	14	10	14	9	16	0	25	16	1	25
2.	Poor working conditions of buses	3	4	2	9	1	1	36	4	25	49
3.	Lengthy legal formalities in case of accidents	2	10	14	7	64	144	25	16	9	49
4.	Targeted route collection	15	1	5	1	196	100	196	16	0	16
5.	Lack of pension schemes for employees	8	7	4	3	1	16	25	9	16	1
6.	Attachment of buses by courts for accident claims	3	10	8	9	49	25	36	4	1	1
7.	Coverage of targeted kilometres per litre of diesel	1	5	3	5	16	4	16	4	0	4
8.	Suspension of employees for accidents	11	7	5	1	16	36	100	4	36	16
9.	Increased work load	10	2	1	9	64	81	1	1	49	64
10.	Lack of co-operation from the general public	11	10	11	7	1	0	16	1	9	16
11.	Cancellation of driving license for accidents	5	10	10	9	25	25	16	0	1	1

12.	Absence of increase in salary in tune with experience	5	5	9	5	0	16	0	16	0	16
13.	Poor family income due to cancellation of driving license	13	3	14	9	100	1	16	121	36	25
14	Vast difference in pay among the employees	7	10	5	9	9	4	4	25	1	16
15.	Lack of motivation by the administration	15	10	12	3	25	9	144	4	49	81
16.	Routes with poor collection	8	9	12	9	1	16	1	9	0	9
	Total					Σd_1^2 **584**	Σd_2^2 **478**	Σd_3^2 **657**	Σd_4^2 **250**	Σd_5^2 **233**	Σd_6^2 **389**

Source : Primary Data

respondents are 'Non-availability of health care facilities', 'Lengthy legal formalities in case of accidents', 'Attachment of buses by courts for accident claims', 'Lack of co-operation from the general public', 'Cancellation of driving licence for accidents', 'Vast difference in pay among the employees' and 'Lack of motivation by the administration'. 'Increased workload' has again become the most important aspect affecting the climate as preferred by the respondents with 21 to 30 years of experience, followed by the aspect 'Poor working conditions of buses' as their next preference. The elements

'Non-availability of health care facilities', 'Lengthy legal formalities in case of accidents' and 'Poor family income due to cancellation of licence' are the least preferred aspects identified by this group as affecting the climate in the organisation. 'Targeted route collection', and 'Suspension of employees for accidents' are the most important aspects identified as affecting the work climate by the respondents with over 30 years of experience. 'Lack of pension schemes for employees' and 'Lack of motivation by the administration' are the elements ranked second by this segment of the respondents.

The least important rank was given by this group of respondents to the aspects other than those of 'Lengthy legal formalities in case of accidents', 'Coverage of targeted kilometres per litre of diesel', 'Lack of co-operation from the general public' and 'Absence of increase in salary on the basis of work experience'.

Table 6.9 shows the relationship among and the correlation between different groups based on work experience on aspects affecting work climate in the organisation. It could be observed that the co-efficient of correlation in ranking the aspects affecting organisational climate is above 0.5 which is high between the respondents who have put in 11-20 and 21-30 years of experience. It should be noted that the co-efficient of correlation is low among the other groups with multiple ranges of work experience.

Table 6.9 : Correlation between the Groups of Respondents with Different Years of Work Experience

Work Experience Group for Analysis	'R' Value	't' Value	'P' Value	Result
Below 10 & 11 to 20 years	-0.11806	-0.44486	0.66322	NS
Below 10 & 21 to 30 years	0.28529	1.11375	0.28414	NS
Below 10 & over 30 years	-0.25944	-1.00514	0.33189	NS
11 to 20 & 21 to 30 years	0.51390	2.24148	0.04172	S
11 to 20 & over 30 years	0.19446	0.74175	0.47050	NS
21 to 30 & over 30 years	0.15708	0.59512	0.56126	NS

Source: Primary Data

A close observation of the 'P' value of groups other than those of the group with 11 to 20 and 21 to 30 years of experience shows that there are differences among them in ranking the different aspects affecting the climate in the organisation.

Table 6.10 shows that the respondents involved in bus operation have chosen 'Lack of pension schemes for employees' as the most important element affecting the climate in the establishment, followed by the element 'Absence of increase in salary in tune with experience' as the second important element preferred by them.

'Non-availability of health care facilities', 'Targeted route collection', 'Attachment of buses by courts for accident claims', 'Poor family income due to cancellation of license', 'Lack of co-operation from the general public', 'Cancellation of driving licence for accidents' and 'Routes with poor collection' are the least important aspects identified by this segment of respondents. As far as the respondents involved in bus maintenance are concerned the first rank was given by them to the aspect 'Lack of pension schemes for employees', and the aspect 'Increased work load' has been preferred as the next factor affecting the work climate in the establishment. The least important aspects identified by this group of respondents as influencing the climate are 'Non availability of health care facilities', 'Lengthy legal formalities in case of accidents', 'Attachment of buses by courts for accident claims', 'Suspension of employees for accidents', 'Lack of co-operation from the general public' and 'Cancellation of driving licence for accidents'. 'Targeted route collection' is the aspect identified by the respondents involved in office administration as the most important element responsible for the existing climate in the organisation, followed by 'Poor working conditions of buses' as the next aspect responsible. The least important element identified by this group of respondents is 'Lack of pension schemes for employees'.

Table 6.11 shows the co-efficient of correlation and the nature of relationship among the respondents who are involved in different jobs. It could be observed that the co-efficient of correlation is high between the groups involved in bus operation and bus maintenance. It should be further noted that the co-efficient of correlation is low among the other groups. A close observation of the 'P' value also enables the researcher to understand that it is below 0.05 between the groups of respondents involved in bus operation and bus maintenance. The table further reveals that the 'P' value is above 0.05 in other groups taken for analysis.

Table 6.12 shows that the respondents who are diploma holders have identified 'Lack of pension schemes for employees' as the prime aspect followed by 'Increased work load' as the next aspect influencing the prevailing organisational climate. The aspects identified by them as the least important are other than those of 'Poor working conditions of buses', 'Targeted route collection', 'Coverage of targeted kilometres per litre of diesel', 'Absence of increase in salary in tune with experience', 'Poor family income due to cancellation of license' and 'Routes with poor collection'. The aspect 'Coverage of targeted kilometre per litre of diesel' has been preferred by the engineering degree holders as the

Table 6.10 : Nature of Job of the Respondents and Aspects Ranked as Affecting the Organisational Climate

Sl.No.	Aspects of Work Life	Number of Job & Ranks					
		Bus operation	Bus maintenance	Office Administration	1&2 d_1^2	1&3 d_2^2	2&3 d_3^2
1	2	3	4	5	6	7	8
1.	Non-availability of health care facilities	13	16	8	9	25	64
1.	Non-availability of health care facilities	10	11	5	1	25	16
2.	Poor working conditions of buses	6	5	2	1	16	9
3.	Lengthy legal formalities in case of accidents	8	11	9	9	1	4
4.	Targeted route collection	10	6	1	16	81	25
5.	Lack of pension schemes for employees	1	1	15	0	196	196
6.	Attachment of buses by courts for accident claims	10	11	5	1	25	36
7.	Coverage of targeted kilometers per litre of diesel	4	3	6	1	4	9
8.	Suspension of employees for accidents	3	11	4	64	1	49

9.	Increased work load	5	2	3	9	4	1
10.	Lack of co-operation from the general public	10	11	11	1	1	0
11.	Cancellation of driving license for accidents	10	11	7	1	9	16
12.	Absence of increase in salary in tune with experience	2	4	13	4	121	81
13.	Poor family income due to cancellation of license	10	7	10	9	0	9
14.	Vast difference in pay among the employees	7	9	8	4	1	1
15.	Lack of motivation by the administration	9	10	13	1	16	9
16.	Routes with poor collection	10	8	11	4	1	9
	Total				**Σd_1^2 126**	**Σd_2^2 502**	**Σd_3^2 470**

Source : Primary Data.

primary and 'Lack of pension schemes for employees' as the secondary aspect that influences the prevailing organisational climate. The least important rank has been given to the aspects other than those of 'Absence of increase in salary in tune with experience' and 'Vast difference in pay among the employees'.

Table 6.11 : Correlation between the Respondents with Difference in Nature of Job

Dependent Groups for Analysis	'R' Value	't' Value	'P' Value	Result
Bus operation & Bus maintenance	0.57218	2.61046	0.02055	S
Bus operation & Office administration	–0.00462	–0.01727	0.98646	NS
Bus maintenance & Office administration	0.07415	0.27822	0.78491	NS

Source: Primary Data.

The respondents who have their educational qualification below Standard XII have chosen ''Targeted route collection' as the most important aspect that affects the climate in the organisation followed by the aspect 'Increased work load'. The least important aspects identified by the same group as influencing the existing organisational climate in the corporation are 'Non-availability of health care facilities' and 'Vast difference in pay among the employees'. 'Coverage of targeted kilometres per litre of diesel' has been identified by the degree holders in Arts and Science as the prime aspect and 'Vast difference in pay among the employees' as the second aspect responsible for the prevailing organisational climate. The least factor identified as standing as a stumbling block against the creation of a conducive organisational climate is 'Lack of motivation by the administration'.

Table 6.13 shows the relationship among and the correlation between the different groups based on the educational qualification of the respondents on aspects affecting work climate in the organisation. The co-efficient of

Table 6.12 : Educational Qualification of the Respondents and Aspects Ranked as Affecting the Organisational Climate

Sl. No.	Aspects of Work Life	Work Experience & Ranks				1&2 d_1^2	1&3 d_2^2	1&4 d_3^2	1&3 d_4^2	1&4 d_5^2	1&5 d_6^2
		Below 10 yrs	31-20 yrs	21-30 yrs	Over 30 yrs						
1	2	3	4	5	6	7	8	9	10	11	12
1.	Non-availability of health care facilities	9	5	15	13	16	36	16	100	64	4
2.	Poor working conditions of buses	3	5	3	3	4	0	0	4	4	0
3.	lengthy legal formalities in case of accidents	9	5	7	11	16	4	4	4	36	16
4.	Targeted route collection	7	5	1	9	4	36	4	16	16	64
5.	Lack of pension schemes for employees	1	2	10	9	1	81	64	64	49	1
6.	Attachment of buses by courts for accident claims	9	5	12	3	16	9	36	49	4	81
7.	Coverage of targeted kilometres per litre of diesel	7	1	5	1	36	4	36	16	8	16
8.	Suspension of employees for accidents	9	5	3	6	16	36	9	4	1	9
9.	Increased work load	2	5	2	5	9	0	9	9	0	9
10.	Lack of co-operation from the general public	9	5	12	12	16	9	9	49	49	0
11.	Cancellation of driving license for accidents	9	5	12	7	16	9	4	49	4	25

12.	Absence of increase in salary in tune with experience	4	3	10	8	1	36	16	49	25	4
13.	Poor family income due to cancellation of driving license	5	5	5	13	0	0	64	0	64	64
14.	Vast difference in pay among the employees	9	4	15	2	25	36	49	121	4	169
15.	Lack of motivation by the administration	9	5	8	16	16	1	49	9	121	64
16.	Routes with poor collection	6	5	8	13	1	4	49	9	64	25
	Total					Σd_1^2 **193**	Σd_2^2 **301**	Σd_3^2 **418**	Σd_4^2 **552**	Σd_5^2 **505**	Σd_6^2 **551**

Source : Primary Data.

correlation is below 0.5 which is low among all the groups with multiple range of educational qualification.

Table 6.13 : Correlation between the Groups of Respondents as per their Educational Qualification

Dependent Groups for Analysis	'R' Value	't' Value	'P' Value	Result
Diploma & Degree in Engineering	0.33459	1.32847	0.20527	NS
Diploma & Below Standard XII	0.47716	2.03158	0.06163	NS
Diploma & Degree in Arts and Science	0.10264	0.38609	0.70523	NS
Degree in Engineering & Below Standard XII	-0.19060	-0.72647	0.47952	NS
Degree in Engineering & Degree in Arts and Science	0.42207	1.74199	0.10343	NS
Below Standard XII &Degree in Engineering	0.10558	0.39725	0.69717	NS

Source : Primary data.

It could also be seen that the 'P' value is greater than the required value of 0.05 and hence the insignificant relationship showing differences among the four status groups in ranking the different aspects affecting organisational climate.

Table 6.14 shows that the respondents who a draw salary between Rs. 5,000 and 8,000 have identified 'Increased work load' as the prime aspect that affects the climate in the organisation, followed by the aspect 'Poor working conditions of buses'. The least important aspect identified by them are 'Non-availability of health care facilities', 'Targeted route collection' and 'Lack of motivation by the administration'. The aspects identified by the respondents receiving a salary ranging between Rs. 8,001 and Rs. 11,000 as affecting the

Table 6.14 : Salary of Respondents and Aspects Ranked as Affecting the Organisational Climate

Sl. No.	Aspects of Work Life	Work Experience & Ranks									
		Below 10 yrs	31-20 yrs	21-30 yrs	Over 30 yrs	1&2 d_1^2	1&3 d_2^2	1&4 d_3^2	1&3 d_4^2	1&4 d_5^2	1&5 d_6^2
1	2	3	4	5	6	7	8	9	10	11	12
	RANKS										
1.	Non-availability of health care facilities	14	10	12	9	16	4	25	4	1	9
2.	Poor working conditions of buses	2	3	6	9	1	16	49	9	36	9
3.	Lengthy legal formalities in case of accidents	3	10	12	7	49	81	16	4	9	25
4.	Targeted route collection	14	1	2	1	169	144	169	1	0	1
5.	Lack of pension schemes for employees	8	1	12	3	49	16	25	121	4	81
6.	Attachment of buses by courts for accident claims	4	10	6	9	36	4	25	16	1	9
7.	Coverage of targeted kilometres per litre of diesel	8	4	1	5	16	49	9	9	1	16
8.	Suspension of employees for accidents	12	8	2	1	16	100	121	36	49	1
9.	Increased work load	1	4	2	9	9	1	64	4	25	49
10.	Lack of co-operation from the general public	12	10	10	7	4	4	25	0	9	9

11.	Cancellation of driving license for accidents	6	10	8	9	16	4	9	4	1	1
12.	Absence of increase in salary in tune with experience	11	6	8	5	25	9	36	4	1	9
13.	Poor family income due to cancellation of driving license	7	7	12	9	0	25	4	25	4	9
14.	Vast difference in pay among the employees	8	9	2	9	1	36	1	49	0	49
15.	Lack of motivation by the administration	14	10	12	3	16	4	121	4	49	81
16.	Routes with poor collection	4	10	11	9	36	49	25	1	1	4
	Total					**Σd_1^2 459**	**Σd_2^2 546**	**Σd_3^2 724**	**Σd_4^2 291**	**Σd_5^2 191**	**Σd_6^2 362**

organisational climate are 'Targeted route collection' and 'Lack of pension schemes for employees' followed by 'Poor working conditions of buses' as the second important aspect. The least important rank is given to the aspects other than those of 'Coverage of targeted kilometres per litre of diesel', 'Suspension of employees for accidents', 'Increased work load', 'Absence of increase in salary in tune with experience', 'Poor family income due to cancellation of licence' and 'Vast difference in pay among the employees'. The respondents whose salary is between Rs. 11,001 and Rs. 14,000 have chosen 'Coverage of targeted kilometres per litre of diesel' as the major aspect affecting the work climate in the study unit. According to them the second major aspects are 'Suspension of employees for accidents' and 'Increased work load'. The least important aspects as identified by them are 'Non-availability of health care facilities', 'Lengthy legal formalities in case of accidents', 'Lack of pension schemes for employees', 'Poor family income due to cancellation of license' and 'Lack of motivation by the administration'. 'Targeted route collection' and 'Suspension of employees for accidents' are the primary aspects identified by the respondents with a salary of over Rs.14000. 'Lack of pension schemes for employees' and 'Lack of Motivation by the administration' are the secondary aspects responsible for the prevailing organisational climate. The least important aspects identified by them are other than those of 'Lengthy legal formalities in case of accidents', 'Coverage of targeted kilometers per litre of diesel', 'Lack of co-operation from the general public' and 'Absence of increase in salary in tune with experience'.

Table 6.15 shows the relationship among and the correlation between the different groups based on salary on aspects affecting the work climate in the organisation. It could be observed that the co-efficient of correlation in ranking the aspects affecting organisational climate is below 0.5 which is low among the different groups with different range of salary except that of the groups receiving salary from Rs. 5,000-8,000 and over Rs. 14,000. A close observation of the 'P' value of the groups other than those of the group with salary Rs. 5,000 and Rs. 8,000 & over Rs. 14,000 shows that the relationship among them is not significant in ranking the different aspects affecting the climate in the organisation.

Table 6.15 : Correlation between the Respondents as per the Range of their Salary

Dependent Groups for Analysis	'R' Value	't' Value	'P' Value	Result
Rs. 5000-8000 & Rs. 8001-11000	0.04182	0.15663	0.87777	NS
Rs. 5000-8000 & Rs. 11001-14000	0.09561	0.35940	0.72466	NS
Rs. 5000-8000 & Over Rs. 14000	-0.60972	-2.87829	0.01215	S
Rs. 8001-11000 & Rs. 11001-14000	0.41741	1.71869	0.10769	NS
Rs. 8001-11000 & Over Rs. 14000	0.34772	1.38763	0.18694	NS
Rs. 11001-14000 & Over Rs.14000	0.09203	0.34581	0.73463	NS

Source: Primary Data.

Table 6.16 shows that the respondents living in nuclear families are of the opinion that 'Targeted route collection' is the first aspect that affects the work climate prevailing in the organisation followed by 'Increased work load' as the second aspect. The least important aspect that influences the status of work climate identified by the same group is 'Non-availability of health care facilities'. The respondents living in joint families are of the opinion that 'Coverage of targeted kilometers per litre of diesel' as the primary aspect responsible for the present status of work climate in the organisation, followed by 'Increased work load'. The least important aspects identified as contributing towards the prevailing organisational climate are 'Lack of motivation by the administration' and 'Routes with poor collection'.

Table 6.16 : Family Status of Respondents and Aspects Ranked as Affecting the Organisational Climate

Sl.No.	Aspects of Work Life	Status & Ranks		$1 \& 2\ d_1^2$
		Married	Unmarried	
1.	Non-availability of health care facilities	16	13	9
2.	Poor working conditions of buses	4	3	1
3.	Lengthy legal formalities in case of accidents	10	11	1
4.	Targeted route collection	1	11	100
5.	Lack of pension schemes for employees	5	4	1
6.	Attachment of buses by courts for accident claims	12	6	36
7.	Coverage of targeted kilometers per litre of diesel	9	1	64
8.	Suspension of employees for accidents	3	8	25
9.	Increased work load	2	2	0
10.	Lack of co-operation from the general public	15	8	49
11.	Cancellation of driving license for accidents	10	8	4
12.	Absence of increase in salary in tune with experience	5	6	1
13.	Poor family income due to cancellation of driving license	7	13	36
14.	Vast difference in pay among the employees	13	5	64
15.	Lack of motivation by the administration	13	15	4
16.	Routes with poor collection	8	15	49
	Total			**Σd_1^2 444**

Source: Primary Data.

Table 6.17 shows the score of rank order correlation and the relationship among the respondents with difference in family status. It is evident from the table that the co-efficient of correlation in ranking the aspects affecting organisational climate is less than 0.5 which is low between the respondents with nuclear and joint family status.

Table 6.17 : Correlation between the Groups of Respondents with Different Family Status

Dependent Groups for Analysis	'R' Value	't' Value	'P' Value	Result
Nuclear & Joint	0.31060	1.22264	0.24165	NS

Source: Primary Data.

It could also be seen that the 'P' value is greater than the required value of 0.05 and hence the insignificant relationship among the two status groups in ranking the different aspects affecting organisational climate.

Table 6.18 shows that 'Increased work load' is identified by the respondents residing in rural areas as the prime aspect responsible for the prevailing work climate in the organisation, followed by 'Targeted route collection'. The aspects identified as least affecting the work climate are 'Lengthy legal formalities incase of accidents', 'Cancellation of driving licence for accidents' and 'Absence of increase in salary in tune with experience'. The respondents residing in urban areas are of the opinion that 'Absence of increase in salary in tune with experience' is the prime aspect responsible for the state of work climate in the organisation and that 'Coverage of targeted kilometres per litre of diesel' is the second important aspect responsible. The least important aspect identified by the same group is 'Non-availability of health care facilities'.

Table 6.18 : Place of Living of Respondents and Aspects Ranked as Affecting the Organisational Climate

Sl.No.	Aspects of Work Life	Status & Ranks		
		Married	Unmarried	1 & 2 d_1^2
1.	Non-availability of health care facilities	11	16	25
2.	Poor working conditions of buses	3	4	1
3.	Lengthy legal formalities in case of accidents	14	8	36
4.	Targeted route collection	2	8	36
5.	Lack of pension schemes for employees	8	3	25
6.	Attachment of buses by courts for accident claims	9	6	9
7.	Coverage of targeted kilometres per litre of diesel	5	2	9
8.	Suspension of employees for accidents	6	5	1
9.	Increased work load	1	14	169
10.	Lack of co-operation from the general public	11	12	1
11.	Cancellation of driving licence for accidents	14	6	64
12.	Absence of increase in salary in tune with experience	14	1	169
13.	Poor family income due to cancellation of driving license	4	15	121
14.	Vast difference in pay among the employees	7	10	9
15.	Lack of motivation by the administration	11	13	4
16.	Routes with poor collection	9	11	4
	Total			Σd_1^2 **683**

Source : Primary Data

Table 6.19 shows that the value of correlation in ranking the different aspects affecting the organisational climate is below 0.5 which is low between the respondents with difference in place of living. The 'P' value is above 0.05 and hence the insignificant relationship among the respondents in weighing the various aspects affecting the climate in the organisation.

Table 6.19 : Correlation between the Groups of Respondents Living in Different Areas

Dependent Groups for Analysis	'R' Value	't' Value	'P' Value	Result
Rural & Urban	-0.06153	-0.23065	0.82092	NS

Source : Primary Data

Table 6.20 shows that 'Targeted route collection' is the prime aspect and 'Increased work load' as the second aspect that affects the organisational climate in the study area as identified by the respondents who have one earning member in their family. The least important aspects responsible are 'Non-availability of health care facilities', 'Lengthy legal formalities incase of accidents', 'Cancellation of driving license for accidents' and 'Lack of motivation by the administration'. 'Lack of pension schemes for employees' is the primary aspect identified by the respondents who have two earning members in their families and the secondary aspects identified are 'Poor working conditions of buses and 'Absence of increase in salary in tune with experience'. The aspects identified as least important for the prevailing organisational work climate are 'Non-availability of health care facilities', 'Lack of co-operation from the general public' and 'Poor family income due to cancellation of licence'. The respondents with three earning members in the family have identified 'Coverage of targeted kilometers per litre of diesel' as the major aspect and 'Increased work load' as the second major aspect that affects the prevailing work climate in the organisation. The least important rank has been given to the aspects other than

Table 6.20 : Number of Earning Members in the Family and Aspects Ranked as Affecting the Organisational Climate

Sl. No.	Aspects of Work Life	Number of Earning Members & Ranks					
		1 or 2	3 or 4	5 or 6	1&2 d_1^2	1&3 d_2^2	2&3 d_3^2
1	2	3	4	5	6	7	8
1.	Non-availability of health care facilities	13	14	8	1	25	36
2.	Poor working conditions of buses	3	2	8	1	25	36
3.	Lengthy legal formalities in case of accidents	13	8	4	25	81	16
4.	Targeted route collection	1	12	4	121	9	64
5.	Lack of pension schemes for employees	8	1	6	49	4	25
6.	Attachment of buses by courts for accident claims	6	10	8	16	4	4
7.	Coverage of targeted kilometres per litre of diesel	5	7	1	4	16	36
8.	Suspension of employees for accidents	6	4	8	4	4	16
9.	Increased work load	2	4	2	4	0	4
10.	Lack of co-operation from the general public	10	14	6	16	16	64

11.	Cancellation of driving license for accidents	13	8	3	25	100	25
12.	Absence of increase in salary in tune with experience	8	2	8	36	0	36
13.	Poor family income due to cancellation of driving licence	4	14	8	100	16	36
14.	Vast difference in pay among the employees	11	6	8	25	9	4
15.	Lack of motivation by the administration	13	12	8	1	25	16
16.	Routes with poor collection	11	10	8	1	9	4
	Total				**Σd_1^2 429**	**Σd_2^2 343**	**Σd_3^2 422**

Source: Primary Data.

those of 'Lengthy legal formalities incase of accidents', 'Targeted route collection', 'Lack of pension schemes for employees', 'Lack of co-operation from the general public' and 'Cancellation of driving license for accidents'.

Table 6.21 shows the relationship among the respondents in viewing the aspects affecting organisational climate together with a varied number of earning members in their families. The co-efficient of correlation in ranking the different aspects affecting the organisational climate is less than 0.5 which is low between the different groups of respondents with varied number of earning members in their families. It could also be seen that the 'P' value is greater than the required value of 0.05 which is not significant.

Table 6.21 : Correlation between the Groups of Respondents with Different Number of Earning Members in the Family

Dependent Groups for Analysis	'R' Value	't' Value	'P' Value	Result
One & Two	0.23991	0.92467	0.37080	NS
One & Three	0.17211	0.65374	0.52387	NS
Two & Three	0.10459	0.39351	0.69987	NS

Source : Primary data

Table 6.22 shows that the respondents with family income below Rs.10,000 have identified 'Poor family income due to cancellation of licence' as the primary aspect, followed by the secondary aspects 'Poor working conditions of buses', 'Attachment of buses by court for accident claims' and 'Increased work load' affecting the work climate in the organisation. The least important aspects identified as affecting the organisational climate are other than those of 'Targeted route collection' , 'Suspension of employees for accidents', 'Lack of co-operation from the general public' and 'Routes with poor collection'. The aspect 'Increased work load' has been ranked first and 'Targeted route collection' as

Table 6.22 : Family Income of Respondents and Aspects Ranked as Affecting the Organisational Climate

Sl. No.	Aspects of Work Life	Total Family Income (in Rs) & Ranks				1&2 d_1^2	1&3 d_2^2	1&4 d_3^2	1&3 d_4^2	1&4 d_5^2	1&5 d_6^2
		Below 10 yrs	31-20 yrs	21-30 yrs	Over 30 yrs						
1	2	3	4	5	6	7	8	9	10	11	12
1.	Non-availability of health care facilities	9	11	16	11	4	49	4	25	0	25
2.	Poor working conditions of buses	2	3	4	5	1	4	9	1	4	1
3.	Lengthy legal formalities in case of accidents	9	11	7	10	4	4	1	16	1	9
4.	Targeted route collection	5	2	9	2	9	16	9	49	0	49
5.	Lack of pension schemes for employees	9	4	2	6	25	49	9	4	4	16
6.	Attachment of buses by courts for accident claims	2	9	8	11	49	36	81	1	4	9
7.	Coverage of targeted kilometres per litre of diesel	9	8	1	2	1	64	49	49	36	1
8.	Suspension of employees for accidents	5	9	11	1	16	36	16	4	64	100
9.	Increased work load	2	1	9	2	1	49	0	64	1	49
10.	Lack of co-operation from the general public	7	14	12	9	49	25	4	4	25	9

(Contd.)

Table 6.22 (Contd.)

1	2	3	4	5	6	7	8	9	10	11	12
11.	Cancellation of driving license for accidents	9	14	4	41	25	25	4	100	9	49
12.	Absense of increase in salary in tune with experience	9	4	3	8	25	36	1	1	16	25
13.	Poor family income due to cancellation of driving license	1	11	12	11	100	121	100	1	0	1
14.	Vast difference in pay among the employees	9	4	6	11	25	9	4	4	49	25
15.	Lack of motivation by the administration	9	14	12	6	25	9	9	4	64	36
16.	Routes with poor collection	7	4	12	11	9	25	16	64	49	1
	Total					**Σd_1^2 368**	**Σd_2^2 557**	**Σd_3^2 316**	**Σd_4^2 391**	**Σd_5^2 326**	**Σd_6^2 405**

Source: Primary Data.

second among aspects affecting the climate in the workplace by the respondents whose family income ranges between Rs. 10,001 to Rs. 16,000. The least elements identified as affecting the work climate in the organisation are 'Lack of co-operation from general public', 'Cancellation of driving license for accidents' and 'lack of motivation by the administration'. The respondents whose total family income ranges between Rs. 16,001 to Rs. 22,000 have identified 'Coverage of targeted kilometers per litre of diesel' as the first aspect fully responsible for the prevailing work climate in the organisation. 'Lack of pension schemes for employees' is the second aspect in rank order. The least important aspect identified as responsible is 'Non-availability of health care facilities'. The respondents who have over Rs. 22,000 as total family income have identified 'Suspension of employees for accidents' as the primary aspect and 'Targeted route collection', 'Coverage of targeted kilometres per litre of diesel' and 'Increased work load' as the secondary aspects responsible for the existing climate in the workplace. The least important rank is given to the aspect 'Cancellation of driving licence for accidents' by the respondents.

Table 6.23 shows that the co-efficient of correlation in ranking the different aspects affecting the organisational climate is less than 0.5 which is low among the different groups of respondents with varied amounts of family income. A close observation of the 'P' value of the different family income groups shows that there are insignificant relationships among them in ranking the different aspects affecting the climate in the organisation.

Summary

An attempt has been taken in this chapter to identify the preference of the respondents on the various aspects affecting organisational climate in the study area.

Table 6.23 : Correlation between the Groups of Respondents with Different Total Family Income

Sl. No.	Age Group for Analysis	'R' Value	't' Value	'P' Value	Result
1.	Below Rs. 10,000 & Rs. 10001 to Rs. 16000	0.30345	1.19158	0.25324	NS
2.	Below Rs. 10,000 & Rs. 16001 to Rs. 22,000	-0.31460	-1.24007	0.23533	NS
3.	Below Rs. 10,000 & Over Rs. 22,000	0.14321	0.54142	0.59673	NS
4.	Rs. 10001 to Rs. 16,000 & Rs. 16,001 to Rs. 22,000	0.36043	1.44577	0.17026	NS
5.	Rs. 10,001 to Rs. 16,000 & Over Rs. 22,000	0.42127	1.73799	0.10415	NS
6.	Rs. 16,001 to Rs. 22,000 & Over Rs. 22,000	0.25694	0.99478	0.33673	NS

Source: Primary Data.

It also shows how the socio-economic profile of the respondents influence their ranking of the different aspects of work life. The chapter further shows the co-efficient of correlation and overall relationship among the different groups of the respondents on the basis of socio-economic factors.

Summary of Findings, Suggestions and Conclusion

Introduction

Organisations like finger prints are always unique. Each has its own culture, traditions and methods of action which in their totality constitute its climate. Some organisations are vibrant and efficient while others are easy going. Some are quite human and others are hard and cold. An organisation tends to attract and keep people who fit its climate so that its patterns are to some extend perpetuated. Just as people may choose to move to a certain geographic climate of the sea, the mountain or desert organisations can also choose the climate they prefer.

The climate available in any organisations should improve its productivity and extend physiological and psychological support to the workforce. Establishments like government undertakings should act as a model to the rest of the business undertakings in the matter of creation and the adherence of an exemplary work climate. Hence, in the present study entitled 'Organisational Climate has been undertaken to find out the nature of the work climate present and to analyse the factors contributing towards the work climate in existence. To be specific, the objectives of the study are:

(*i*) To find out the perception of employees towards the various dimensions of organisational climate.

(*ii*) To study the relationship between the perception and socio-economic factors of employees.

(*iii*) To identify the influence of organisational climate on motivation and performance of employees.

(*iv*) To examine the relationship between the perception and the understanding of the basic job requisites possessed by the employees.

(*v*) To know the preference of employees over the different aspects of work life which have an impact on organisational climate.

SUMMARY OF FINDINGS

Perception of Organisational Climate

Socio-economic Profile of the Respondents

It has been identified that out of the sample of 300 respondents, 35 per cent of the respondents are in 31 to 40 years age group and the next age group 41 to 50 years also comprises 35 per cent of the respondents. It has been learnt from the study that 70 per cent of the respondents are married and only 30 per cent of them are unmarried. The study further shows that 50 percent of the respondents have a dependents strength of one or two in their families and the three or four dependents category has 35 per cent of the respondents. Thirty-five per cent of the respondents have a work experience which ranges between 21 and 30 years and another 30 per cent of the respondents have below 10 years of work experience. It has been identified in the study that 60 per cent of the respondents are involved in bus operation and the respondents engaged in bus maintenance are 26.7 per cent.

The educational qualification of 40 percent of the respondents is upto standard XII. Forty per cent of the respondents are degree holders in Arts or Science. The study also reveals that 35 per cent of the respondents draw a salary between Rs. 5,000 and 8,000. Thirty per cent of the respondents draw a salary ranging between Rs. 8,001 and 11,000. It has been learnt that, out of the 300 respondents selected for the study, 60 per cent are in the nuclear family setup and the remaining 40 per cent are in joint families. It has been learnt in the study that 60 per cent of the respondents are hailing from urban areas and only 40 per cent of them are from rural areas. Fifty percent of the respondents have two earning members in their families and the families with one earning member account for 40 per cent of the respondents. The study also shows that 40 per cent of the respondents have their family income between Rs. 16,001 and 22,000 and 25 per cent of the respondents have their family income between Rs. 10,001 and 16,000.

Cronbach's Alpha Test of Reliability

Cronbach's Alpha test used to measure the internal consistency and reliability of different items in a scale has shown that the dimension 'Events and Celebration' has the maximum reliability score of 0.909 followed by the dimension 'Management Behaviour' with the second maximum reliability score of 0.904. The least score of reliability has been obtained by the dimension 'Goal Clarity and Acceptance' with a score of 0.758. The dimension 'Work group co-operation friendliness and warmth has the second least reliability score 0.769.

Organisational Climate Perception of the Respondents

Work expectations are properly understood by the employees has been viewed as the dominant aspect under the dimension 'Goal clarity and acceptance' supported by a higher perception score of 1031. As far as the dimension 'Working conditions' is concerned, providing of adequate facilities for ventilation, lighting etc., in the work place has been identified as an important statement with a higher perception score of 805 among the statements given under the dimension. Feeling happier and proud when recognised by the superior and the Management has been viewed as the most preferred aspect with a perception score of 854 under the dimension 'Recognition and satisfaction'.

A higher perception score of 778 obtained by the statement that subordinates are willing to approach the superiors and the superiors are ready to help the subordinates shows that it is a highly preferred statement among the statements given under the dimension 'Work group co-operation, friendliness and warmth'. The statement that the job is challenging and it demands skill and experience has been identified as the most preferred among the various statements given under the dimension 'Job importance, challenge and variety' supported by a higher perception score of 716. It has been identified that the statement belated communication given by the Management does not affect the personal work of employees is the dominant statement among the ones included under the dimension 'Participation and communication' supported by a higher perception score of 756.

As far as the dimension 'Rules and policies' is concerned, the higher perception score of 787 has been obtained by the statement that the recruitment policy of the Corporation ensures a balanced distribution of employment opportunity to all the employees. A higher perception score of 677 has been identified for the statement that the employees are determined to complete the work given at any cost under the dimension 'Employee commitment'. The statement that the work performance of employees is in accordance with the goals of the Corporation has been viewed as the most preferred statement among the ones given under the dimension 'Conflict and Pressure' supported by a higher perception score of 781.

The statement that the Management is fair in sharing information and resources with the employees has been identified as the dominant statement among the various statements given under the dimension 'Fairness', supported by a higher perception score of 768. It has been revealed that opportunities are given equally in the Corporation among the employees to identify their latent skills under the dimension 'Opportunity for growth, innovation and change' supported by a higher perception score of 709. As far as the dimension 'Social values and beliefs' is concerned, the statement that employees are ready to promote harmony in the work place has been identified as the most important among a group of statements given under this dimension. The higher perception score of 1140 is an evidence in this regard.

A higher perception score of 920 obtained by the statement that work is an opportunity given to the employees and it is carried out devotedly shows the importance of the statement in comparision to the other statements included under the dimension 'Professional and Organisational esprit'. The statement that the Management is not using its power to resolve differences in issues has been viewed by the respondents as more important than the other statements included under the dimension 'Management behaviour', supported by a higher perception score of 751.

Under the dimension 'Events and celebrations' a higher perception score of 965 has been identified for the statements that celebrations help to close the differences with fellow employees and to work happily. The statement that discrimination is not found among the employees on the basis of economical status has been viewed as the dominant aspect with a higher perception score of 863 included under the dimension 'Non-work related factors of organisational climate'. The vertical analysis of the different tables showing various dimensions of organisational climate further shows that the respondents have opted different responses viz., 'Undecided (UD)' in eight dimensions, 'Disagree (DA)' in seven dimensions and 'Agree (A)' in only one dimension of organisational climate.

The Mean and Standard Deviation of the Various Dimensions of Organisational Climate

It has been identified that the dimension 'Non-work related factors' has the highest mean value of 26.30 followed by the dimension 'Social values and beliefs' with the second highest mean value of 20.75. The lowest mean value of 12.70 has been obtained for the dimension 'Management behaviour' preceeded by the dimension 'Employee commitment' with the second lowest mean value of 12.80. The mean values thus have expressed the collective view of the respondents on the dimensions of organisational climate. A higher mean value expresses the overall higher preference of the dimension by a majority of the respondents and vice versa.

Level of Perception

The overall highest perception score has been found for the dimension 'Social values and belief' identified by 210 (70%) respondents out of the 300 respondents chosen for the present study. The dimension 'Goal clarity and acceptance' has the highest overall moderate perception score identified by 72 (24%) respondents.

The overall lowest perception score has been found for the dimension 'Conflict and pressure' identified by 268 (89.3%) respondents out of the 300 respondents selected for the study.

Impact of Socio-economic Factors on Perception

It has been identified that the age of the respondents has influenced their perception of the various dimensions of organisational climate in fifteen dimensions. The role of marital status in influencing the perception of the dimensions of organisational climate has been identified in eleven dimensions out of the sixteen dimensions identified for the present study.

The numerical strength of the dependents in the families of the respondents has influenced their perception of twelve out of the sixteen dimensions included for the study. The influence of work experience on the perception of the respondents has been noticed in all the sixteen dimensions identified for the study.

Significant contribution of the nature of the job is found as influencing the perception of the respondents in ten out of the sixteen dimensions. The role of educational qualification has been identified as influencing the respondents' perception in all the sixteen dimensions of organisational climate.

It has been noted that the salary received by the respondents has influenced their perception of fourteen out of the sixteen dimensions identified and included for the present study. The family status of the respondents has influenced their perception of thirteen out of the sixteen dimensions included for the study.

It has been understood that the place of living of the respondents has influenced their perception in eight dimensions of organisational climate out of the sixteen identified for the study. The earning members in the families of the respondents have influenced their perception in fifteen dimensions of organisational climate.

It has been learnt that the family income of the respondents has played a vital role in influencing their perception in all the sixteen dimensions of organisational climate.

Influence of Organisational Climate

Respondents' perception of the influence of Organisational Climate on motivation and Performance

Among the different statements included to find out the influence of Organisational climate on motivation and performance, the highest total score of 964 has been obtained by the statement that the prevailing work climate encourages the workers to maintain team spirit in the place of work. The second highest total score of 920 has been received by the perception statement that the respondents have never dwelled on their weaknesses and the work atmosphere in the workplace is the main reason for the same.

It has been learnt that the first least score of 445 has been obtained by the statement that the respondents prefer to take up new assignments because of the encouragive work atmosphere present in the corporation. The prevailing human relations has helped the respondents to recover from the setbacks in performance and this view has been supported by the second least score of 571. The vertical analysis of the table with various responses further shows that the respondents have opted 'Disagree (DA)' as the general response, supported by the highest score of 3840, to the initiative of finding out the influence of organisational climate on motivation and performance.

Level of perception of the Influence of Organisational Climate on motivation and Performance

It has been learnt through the analysis that 136 (45.3%) respondents have a high level of perception of the statement that the prevailing work climate encourages the workers to maintain team spirit in the place of work. A moderate level of perception has been found out for the statement that the work is completed everyday on account of the supportive work environment and the same statement has a score of 78 (26%). The statement that the respondents prefer to take up new assignments because the work atmosphere encourages them has a low perception score of 266 (88.7%).

Correlation between the Dimensions of Organisational Climate and Motivation & Performance

The correlation analysis reveals that there is low correlation among the majority of the dimensions of organisational climate (Dimensions 1, 3, 5, 6, 7, 8, 10, 11, 12, 13, 15, 16) and the motivation and performance score obtained. It has also been learnt that there is negative correlation between the dimensions of organisational climate and the motivation and performance score (Dimensions 2, 9, 14). The correlation between the motivation and performance score and the dimension of organisational climate has been found to be high in only one dimension (Dimension 4).

Respondents' Perception of the Possession of Basic Job Requisites

Among the various statements included to identify the respondents' perception of the possession of basic job requisites, the highest score of 1134 has been obtained by the statement that the respondents believe that they possess the required knowledge to do the job. The perception of respondents further shows that the second highest score of 1130 has been obtained by the statement that the job decisions are implemented by the respondents without any deviation.

The study also shows that the respondents have given the first least score of 520 to the perception statement that they are ready to increase their efficiency in the job. The perception of the respondents regarding the possession of basic job requisites further shows that they are ready to accept more difficult than simple jobs and the same has been supported by the second least score of 638. The vertical analysis of the table with various responses further shows that the respondents have opted 'Strongly Agree (SA)' as their general response, supported by a higher score of 4192, to the imitative of finding out the respondents' perception of the possession of basic job requisites.

Level of Respondents' Perception of the Possession of Basic Job Requisites

It has been identified through the analysis that 214 (71.4%) respondents have high level perception of the statement that a satisfactory level of performance is maintained in the job. The statement of the respondents that the first priority in the work place is to do the job has a moderate level perception, supported by a score of 106 (35.3%). A low level perception has been identified by the statement that the respondents are ready to increase their efficiency in the job and the same statement has a score of 283 (94.3%).

Correlation between the Dimensions of Organisational Climate and the Possession of Basic Job Requisites

An attempt to identify the correlation between the respondents' perception of the dimensions of Organisational climate and the possession of basic job requisites by the respondents has shown that there is low correlation among the majority of the dimensions of Organisational climate (Dimensions 1, 2, 3, 5, 6, 8, 12, 13, 14, 15, 16). It has also been identified that there is negative correlation among the dimensions of Organisational climate (Dimensions 7, 9, 10) and the basic job requisites score. The study further shows that the correlation between the basic job requisites score and the dimensions of Organisational climate is positive in two dimensions (Dimensions 4, 11). The table also shows that the overall correlation between the dimensions of organisational climate and the possession of basic job requisites is low as the score 0.2736 is low than the required score of 0.5.

Preference Over the different Aspects of Work Life

Weighted Scores and Overall Ranks of Aspects Affecting the Organisational Climate

The weighted scores and the overall ranks on aspects affecting the organisational climate shows that the first rank has been given to the aspect 'Increased work load' followed by 'Targeted route collection' getting the second rank in influencing the prevailing work environment in the establishment. The third rank has been given to the aspect 'Coverage of targeted kilometres per litre of diesel'. The least rank has been given to the aspect 'Non-availability of health care facilities' preceeded by 'Lack of motivation by the administration' as the second least aspect contributing towards the prevailing work climate in the Corporation. The third least rank has been given to the aspect 'Lack of co-operation from the general public' as affecting greatly the work environment.

Age of the Respondents and Aspects Ranked as Affecting the Organisational Climate

The element 'Vast difference in pay among the employees' has been identified by the respondents who are below 30 years of age as the prime aspect influencing the climate in the Corporation. The respondents who are 31-40 years of age have indicated 'Increased work load' as the major aspect affecting the Organisational climate.

'Poor working conditions of buses' is the most important element identified by the respondents who are 41 to 50 years of age, as contributing greatly towards the prevailing work climate. The elements 'Poor working conditions of buses' and 'Suspension of employees for accidents' have been identified by the respondents of the age group over 50 as the significant forces playing a vital role in the work climate existing in the Corporation.

Correlation between the different age groups of respondents

The Co-efficient of correlation among the different age groups in identifying the different aspects affecting organisational climate is low. The low 'P' value among the different age groups reveals that the relationship among them is not significant in viewing the different aspects affecting Organisational climate.

Status of the respondents and aspects ranked as affecting the Organisational Climate

The married segment of the respondents have identified 'Targeted route collection' as the basic element responsible for the current work climate in the Corporation. 'Suspension of employees for accidents' has been identified by the unmarried group of respondents as the vital element contributing towards the Organisational climate.

Correlation between the different status groups of respondents

A low Co-efficient of correlation has been found between the married and unmarried groups of respondents in weighing the aspects affecting the work climate in the Corporation. The relationship between the married and unmarried groups of respondents in viewing at the different aspects affecting the work climate is not significant.

Number of dependents in the family of the respondents and aspects ranked as affecting the Organisational Climate

The respondents with below two dependents in the family have identified 'Increased work load' as the important aspect that affects the work climate in the Corporation. The aspect 'Poor working condition of buses' has been identified by the respondents with 3 to 4 dependents as the issue that influences the Organisational climate. The respondents with 5 to 6 dependents are of the opinion that 'Coverage of targeted kilometers per litre of diesel' has been the major contributor to the work climate prevailing in the Corporation.

Correlation between the different dependent groups of respondents

The Co-efficient of correlation is low among the different groups of respondents with varied number of dependents in identifying the different aspects influencing the Organisational climate. The relationship among the respondents with different number of dependents in viewing the elements responsible for the prevailing climate in the Corporation is not significant.

Work experience of the respondents and aspects ranked as affecting the climate in the Corporation

The respondents who have below 10 years of experience have identified 'Coverage of targeted kilometers per litre of diesel' as the major factor affecting the work climate in the establishment. 'Targeted route collection' has been identified by the respondents with 11 to 20 years of experience as the first aspect that affects the Organisational work environment. The aspect 'Increased work load' has been considered by the respondents who have 21 to 30 years of work experience as the important factor that affects the prevailing climate in the Corporation. The respondents possessing experience over 30 years have considered 'Targeted route collection' and 'Suspension of employees for accidents' as prime elements affecting Organisational climate.

Correlation between the groups of respondents with different years of work experience

A low Co-efficient of correlation has been found among the groups of respondents with different years of work experience in viewing the various elements affecting the work environment in the Corporation. A high co-efficient of correlation has been found between the respondents who have put in 11 to 20 and 21 to 30 years of experience in assessing the various aspects affecting the work climate. Insignificant relationship has been identified among the respondents except those of the respondents with 11 to 20 and 21 to 30 years of experience in assessing the various aspects of work environment in the Corporation.

Nature of job of the respondents and aspects ranked as affecting the Organisational climate

The respondents involved in bus operation have ranked the aspect 'Lack of pension schemes for employees' as the important factor which affects the work environment in the Corporation. The factor 'Lack of pension schemes for employees' has been identified by the respondents employed in bus maintenance as contributing primarily towards the work situation in the Corporation. The first rank has been extended to the aspect 'Targeted route collection' by the respondents involved in office administration as affecting the overall work environment in the Corporation.

Correlation between the groups of respondents with difference in nature of job

The value of co-efficient of correlation is low among the majority of the respondents involved in various operations of the establishment in locating the different aspects affecting Organisational climate. Insignificant relationship has been identified among the majority of the respondents employed in different kinds of work in evaluating the various elements contributing towards the work situation.

Educational qualification of the respondents and aspects ranked as affecting the Organisational climate

The respondents who are diploma holders are of the opinion that the aspect 'Lack of pension schemes for employees' affects primarily the climate in the Corporation. The aspect 'Coverage of targeted kilometers per litre of diesel' has been viewed by the degree holders in engineering as the major contributor to the work climate prevailing in the establishment. The respondents with educational qualification below standard XII have found the aspect 'Targeted route collection' as primarily responsible for the existing work environment. 'Coverage of targeted kilometers per litre of diesel' has been identified by the degree holders as an important aspect contributing to the present state of work climate in the Corporation.

Correlation between the groups of respondents as per their educational qualification

A low co-efficient of correlation has been found among the respondents with different educational qualification in looking at the various aspects affecting the organisational climate. The relationship among the respondents with variations in their educational qualification is not significant in viewing the aspects responsible for the work environment present in the Corporation.

Salary of respondents and aspects ranked as affecting the Organisational climate

The respondents with salary between Rs.5,000 and Rs. 8,000 have identified 'Increased work load' as the major aspect that affects the work situation in the establishment. 'Targeted route collection' and 'Lack of pension schemes for employees' are the important aspects identified as responsible for the present state of job climate in the Corporation as found out by the respondents with salary between Rs. 8,001 and Rs.11,000. The respondents with salary between Rs. 11,001 and Rs. 14,000 have identified 'Coverage of targeted kilometers per litre of diesel' as the major aspect contributing to the work climate in the Corporation. The two major aspects identified out by the respondents who are receiving the salary over Rs.14000 are 'Targeted route collection' and 'Suspension of employees for accidents'.

Correlation between the respondents as per the range of their salary

The co-efficient of correlation is low among the various groups of respondents with difference in their salary level in judging the various aspects affecting the work climate in the establishment except that of the respondents whose salaries are below Rs.5,000 and Rs. 8,000 and over Rs.14,000. Insignificant relationship has been identified among the various respondents with difference in their salary levels in identifying the various aspects affecting the work climate in the establishment except that of the respondents whose salary level is between Rs.5,000 and Rs. 8,000 and over Rs.14,000.

Family status of respondents and aspects ranked as affecting the Organisational climate

The respondents who have nuclear families have identified the aspect 'Targeted route collection' as contributing greatly the existing climate in the establishment. 'Coverage of targeted kilometres per litre of diesel' is the aspect identified by the respondents with joint families as being primarily responsible for the present state of job climate in the Corporation.

Correlation between the groups of respondents with different family status

The co-efficient of correlation is low among the respondents who have nuclear and joint families in viewing the various aspects responsible for the work climate prevailing in the establishment. The relationship among the respondents with different kinds of family grouping is not significant in viewing the different aspects affecting the work climate in the Corporation.

Place of living of respondents and aspects ranked as affecting the Organisational climate

The respondents who are living in the rural area have identified the aspects 'Increased work load' as the prime force affecting the climate in the Corporation. The aspect 'Absence of increase in salary on the basis of experience' has been viewed by the respondents hailing from urban locations as the major factor contributing the prevailing work climate in the establishment.

Correlation between the groups of respondents living in different areas

The co-efficient of correlation is low among the respondents coming from rural and urban locations in viewing the various aspects affecting the climate in the Corporation. Insignificant relationship has been found among the various groups of respondents hailing from various locations like rural and urban areas in viewing the various aspects contributing greatly to the climate in the establishment.

Number of earning members in the family and aspects ranked as affecting Organisational climate

'Targeted route collection' is the aspect found to contribute to a great level to the prevailing work climate in the Corporation as identified by the respondents who have one earning member in their families. The respondents who have two earning members in their families have identified 'Lack of pension schemes for employees' as the major aspect influencing the work climate in the establishment. 'Coverage of targeted kilometers per litre of diesel' has been identified as the major force responsible for the work climate prevailing in the Corporation by the respondents who have three earning member in their families.

Correlation between the groups of respondents with different number of earning members in the family

The co-efficient of correlation is low among the respondents with different number of earning members in their families in identifying the different aspects affecting the climate in the establishment. The relationship among the respondents with varied number of earning members in their families is not significant in viewing the different aspects responsible for the existing state of climate in the establishment. This insignificant relationship shows that the number of earning members present in the families of respondents has influenced their ranking of the aspects affecting the Organisational climate.

Family income of respondents and aspects ranked as affecting the Organisational climate

'Poor family income due to cancellation of licence' is the aspect identified by the respondents whose family income is below Rs.10,000 as the prime factor affecting the prevailing work climate in the Corporation. The respondents with a total family income between Rs.10,001 and Rs.16,000 have identified the aspect 'Increased work load' as affecting greatly the prevailing work situation in the establishment. The first rank has been extended to the aspect 'Coverage of targeted kilometres per litre of diesel' by the respondents whose total family income is between Rs.16,001 and Rs.22,000. The aspect 'Suspension of employees for accidents' has been chosen by the respondents whose total family income is over Rs.22,000 as the major aspect that influences the work environment in the establishment.

Correlation between the groups of respondents with different total family income

The co-efficient of correlation is low among the respondents with difference in total family income in identifying the various aspects affecting the work climate in the establishment. The relationship among the respondents with different total family income is not significant in viewing the different aspects responsible for the present state of climate in the Corporation.

SUGGESTIONS

To Improve the Perception of the Employees Towards the Various Dimensions of Organisational Climate

1. Goal Clarity and Acceptance

It has been learnt that the employees in the Corporation have a clear idea of what is actually expected of them in terms of their work performance and of what the goal of the Corporation is. While there is an awareness, there are also certain misconceptions among the stakeholders about the possibility of its attainment, the amount of energy to be devoted, fixing up of responsibilities on people for its attainment and non-attainment, possible increase of pressure when still better goals are set and achievements are demanded and finally on the share of the fruit that is going to be enjoyed by the work force in the event of its attainment. Hence there is a poor and unwilling acceptance of employees towards the work goals set by the Management.

Suggestions

In order to clear the misconceptions, especially on the part of the employees the following suggestions are offered for consideration :

(*a*) the employees should be involved in the goal setting process of the individuals and the Corporation.

(*b*) the assurances given by the management for the betterment of the work force in the event of the organisational and individual goal attainment should be fulfilled.

(*c*) the work force of the Corporation should also come forward to expend their energy for goal attainment, taking into account the threats arising as a result of their non co-operation and eventually making the Corporation financially sick.

Working conditions

The working conditions prevailing in Tamil Nadu State Transport Corporation, Tirunelveli District can be classified into physical and psychological. The physical working conditions surrounding the job are favourable in general and not favourable in particular, especially with regard to work load. There is no doubt that the employees in the Corporation are aware of the Organisational and individual goals. While the clarity in understanding of goals is accepted , it has been found out that there is reduced motivation in the workforce for its attainment. As per the understanding between the employees and the Management of the Corporation, an employee should work for 8 hours per day to complete a single duty. But it has been found out that the drivers and conductors are compelled to work beyond 10 hours per day and they are made to operate the buses day and night to cover 900 kms in double or even triple duties. As per the motor employees act, a worker should be given 9 hours of rest between two single duties and it is seen that this ruling is also not followed closely in the Corporation. The result is that the physical and mental condition of the drivers and conductors are affected which ultimately leads to frequent road accidents, loss of life and property, compliance with lengthy legal formalities, increased accident claims by the victims, suspension of driving licenses and a poor state of the family income of employees.

SUGGESTIONS

In order to overcome this problem, it may be suggested that:

(*a*) scientific determination of work load be done after taking into account the condition of roads and increased road traffic.

(*b*) the strength of employees be increased in proportion to the number of new bus routes included and additional buses added .

(*c*) in the process of calculating the wheel rotation time to arrive at a single duty of 8 hours, the time spent by the employees for sign on and sign off and for consumption of food and rest should be included. A period of 2 hours spent on these activities including the bus halt time allowances should be taken into account in the calculation of wheel rotation time and thereby allowing for a single duty of 6 hours.

Recognition and satisfaction

The status of recognition extended to the employees of the Corporation and the satisfaction derived by the work force out of that are found to be poor in the Corporation. The competitive environment today calls for identifying and implementing strategies for retaining the able work force and there by attempting to expand its horizons in terms of market share and profitability. The Corporation as the result of shifting itself from the carrot to stick approach believes that extension of recognition is not a useful exercise. The only existing mode of extending non-monetary recognition is by differentiating the drivers and conductors who have put in 15 years of service by the distinctive colour of their uniform while they are on duty. It has been found out that promotions among the administrative staff are given by personal and political influences and not purely on the basis of seniority.

SUGGESTIONS

With a view to overcome the poor condition prevailing in extending recognition and gaining satisfaction, it may be suggested that :

(*a*) the Management should first of all develop its faith in extending recognition to the work force.

(*b*) it should identify the different modes through which employees can be recognised in the Corporation when their performance exceeds the standards fixed already.

(*c*) higher involvement and co-operation be shown by the work force in identifying and implementing different recognition plans taking into account the ground realities.

Work group co-operation, friendliness and warmth

The internal and external integration of employees which is a sign of mutual co-operation, friendliness and warmth among the employees in the Corporation is found to be satisfactory. The underlying force that unites the employees involved in bus operation, maintenance and office maintenance is the increasing work pressure mounted upon them and the minimum standards of performance fixed by the Management of the Corporation arbitrarily. This has increased the awareness among the work force to stand united and fight against any of the changes introduced which are detrimental to their physical and mental health. It has been noted that the nature of the work involving the displacement of employees continuously for a period of 10 to 12 hours and the physical and mental strain experienced out of that has made the employees, especially those in bus operation, to return home immediately as soon as the buses reach for halt in the depots. They find limited chances to meet and interact among themselves regularly and thereby promote friendliness and warmth among them.

Suggestions

In order to promote co-operation, friendliness and warmth among the employees of the Corporation it may be suggested that

(a) the work force should be made to realise that they should come united not only to pressurise the Management to yield to their demands but also to help the management of the Corporation to address the problems like continuous financial loss to the Corporation, increase in the cost of maintenance and the price of fuel, alarming increase in the number of accidents and the financial claims to be settled to the victims.

(b) the management of the Corporation should have a positive approach towards the idea of promoting unity among their work force and such integration should not be treated by the Management as a threat to the Corporation.

(c) as an attempt to bring out co-operation, friendliness and warmth among the work force, the management and employees' unions can organise meetings, get-togethers and celebrations; and the unions should educate their members on the need for being united with one another and with the Management of the Corporation to face the present and future challenges.

5. Job importance, challenge and variety

The amount of involvement shown by an employee in a job depends on the physiological and psychological readiness possessed by him. More specifically the psychological readiness of an employee depends on what he gets from a job in terms of salary, status, variety, fringe benefits, challenge involved, working hours and above all the relative rank or position of the job in terms of other jobs available in the Corporation. In the present study, it has been learnt that the employees are aware of the relative importance of the job that they do and a majority of them find that the job is too challenging and detrimental to their physical and mental health. A real challenge is faced by them in their job on the issues such as the coverage of 6 km/litre of diesel (from the previous standard of 4.5 km/litre of diesel), integration of the expectations of the commuters regarding good speed while traveling against the expectation of the Management to cover an additional target of 1.5 km/litre of diesel, excessive pressure from the Management to increase the bus route collection per day, poor operating condition of the buses due to improper maintenance and the use of substandard spare parts , alarming increase in work load to the level of attending double and sometimes triple duties covering 900 km at a stretch by operating the bus day and night without adequate rest, finding fault with the drivers alone for all the road accidents and leaving them jobless etc. In such a situation the employees of the Corporation are not found to be ready to take extra risk by looking for variety in their jobs.

Suggestions

On the basis of the conditions prevailing over the issues aforesaid, it may be suggested that :

1. the management of the Corporation should seriously consider the genuine concerns of the employees and keep them away from the threats they find in their jobs.

2. variety in operations can be encouraged by allotting day and night shifts on voluntary basis and by changing the route operation from one destination to another.
3. the work force should also be made to realise that the overall condition of the Corporation is becoming poor year by year due to the increase in the cost of fuel, the payment of interest on borrowings by the Corporation and continuous financial loss in its operations. In such a situation they have to realise the importance of their role in redeeming the Corporation from its poor functioning by increasing their overall contribution towards the welfare of the Corporation.

Participation and communication

The two ingredients that are necessary for Corporation which is willing to grow are the involvement extended by its work force and a free exchange of communication between the Management and the work force. The prevailing situation in the Corporation enables to understand that most of the decisions concerning the employees like fixation of work load, targets for bus route collection, coverage of stipulated kilometers per litre of diesel and suspension of employees from work for accidents leading to the death of victims are taken unilaterally and hence the poor participation of the work force in the overall functioning of the Corporation. The belated communication given, though it does not affect the personal work of most of the employees, has an impact on the quality of work completed and makes difficult to strike a proper balance between the activities involved in personal and professional life.

SUGGESTIONS

With a view to improve the existing condition as regards participation and communication, it may be suggested that

(*a*) the Management should realise that some of the problems like increase in the efficiency of the Corporation in terms of avoiding financial losses and covering targeted kilometres per litre of diesel are still matters of dispute and that to improve the willing participation of its workforce an amicable solution should be reached by having rounds of discussion with representatives of the work force.

(*b*) involvement of the employees of the Corporation can be increased by devoting enough attention to long pending demands like doing away with any curtailment of the financial benefits already extended and enjoyed by the employees, and taking a humanitarian approach in dealing with certain matters like providing alternative employment to the divers of the Corporation in its own premises in the event of judicial enquiries pending against them in courts of law, especially in cases related to death of victims in accidents.

(*c*) a free flow of communication between the management and employees represented by their respective unions may be realised and as far as possible, modern facilities available for effective and speedy communication should be used for timely passing of information and scheduled attainment of task with perfection.

Rules and policies

Ethical conduct of business supported by a set of rules and regulations and a standing plan always leads an establishment to long standing success in the field of business with advancement in its operations and with name and fame in the market. The prevailing rules and policies in the Corporation are found to be lopsided protecting the interest of the Corporation at the cost of the welfare of its own work force, for example, the rules concerning the manner in which road accidents are treated and how the drivers involved in accidents leading to death of victims are denied work in the Corporation until the case is settled judicially. An another example for lopsided rules and regulations not favourable to its own employees is that relating to fixation of responsibility for poor collection in bus route operation. In the case before in the Supreme Court between *Saran Singh & others* vs *RSRTC & others*, 3003(3) CLR886, the ruling given by the apex court clearly states that bus conductors should not be made responsible for the route collection being lower that fixed by the Management and departmental action should not be initiated against such conductors in the event of poor collection in bus operation.

Suggestions

In view of the status and the application of the existing rules and policies, it may be recommended that

(*a*) the Management should conduct a thorough revision of the rules and policies in force and it has to be ensured that they are consistent with the prevailing conditions of job and free from partiality affecting the interests of a group at the cost of another.

(*b*) the Management should ensure that the application of rules does not vary from person to person based on their membership in unions and their strength in bargaining.

(*c*) the policies of the Corporation should be framed taking into account its long term consequences.

Employee commitment

There are fundamental aspects in jobs which have to be attended immediately and one such important aspect is the overall involvement shown by the workforce. The present status in the Corporation as regards the commitment shown by the employees in their work is not favourable. Though the findings under this dimension show the presence of employee commitment, the same cannot be technically viewed as a natural and spontaneous involvement in work, but rather as a sign of frustration and insecurity coupled with fear of loss and the adverse consequences as the result of its non-compliance.

Suggestions

With a view to enhance the commitment that ought to the shown by the employees in their work, it may be suggested that :

(*a*) the Management should initiate employee confidence building measures such as discussing the actual financial position of the Corporation with the representatives of employees and the ways and means of overcoming various problems concerning the work force and the management of the Corporation. Meetings of the employees enabling them to present their ideas over the issues affecting the Corporation can also be organised to enrich the existing commitment found among the employees.

(*b*) the management should extend recognition and incentives for outstanding achievements in diesel conservation, accident free driving and increased route collection.

(*c*) the management should organise various self awareness and self development programmes enabling the work force to identify self and others and thereby grow as duty bound, responsible and committed employees of the Corporation.

Conflict and pressure

As conflict and pressure are common in the personal lives of individuals, Corporation and its work force also cannot avoid the same in the process of integrating the divergent needs of the employer and employees. There are Corporations today looking for employees who can handle the business pressure so tactically. The present situation in the study unit also reveals that there are unresolved issues of conflict between the Management of the Corporation and the employees in areas like fixation of responsibility for the poor financial performance of the Corporation, arriving at a decision on work load, curtailment of financial benefits extended to the employees for the sake of reducing the expenses, punishments for the different types of offences committed, retirement benefits like gratuity, etc.,. The symptoms of pressure are found explicitly in compelling the running staff to increase the bus route collection and in making the employees to work, day and night even at the cost of their health and the interest of their families.

SUGGESTIONS

In order to overcome the prevailing situation where conflicts and pressure are mounting, it may be recommended that :

(*a*) the issues involving dispute should first of all be mutually identified and agreed upon and initiatives should be taken earnestly in this direction by the management of the Corporation.

(*b*) a scientific cum humanitarian approach should be applied in resolving disputes over issues and both the management and the employees should develop faith among each other in this regard. Proper attention should be given by the Management to implement the various decisions for which settlement has been arrived at earlier.

Fairness

Adherence to fairness in personal and professional life helps for the creation of an orderly society. As far as the existence and adherence to fairness in Tamil Nadu State Transport Corporation, Tirunelveli District is concerned, the situation is alarming and there are issues where the workforce is of the opinion that a just and fair approach is totally absent. Various issues like compelling the staff in the administrative section to attend night duties, taking the wheel rotation time as the base for calculating the working hours, reducing the availability of technical staff from 1.25 per bus to 0.75 per bus and again the availability of administrative staff from 0.75 per bus to 0.35 per bus, improper handling of money deducted from the salary of employees for payment to co-operative societies, outsourcing of job in the Corporation like bus cleaning, canteen maintenance and providing security through the appointment of private security guards are quoted as examples for the poor state of fairness in the Corporation.

Suggestions

The following are the suggestions to improve the applicability of fairness in the Corporation:

(*a*) the management should change their overall approach towards the workforce and it should concentrate equally the welfare of the employees as like looking at it own financial welfare.

(*b*) the management of the Corporation should implement the various mutually agreed settlements reached between the employer (The Government of Tamil Nadu, represented by the Minister for Transport) and the representatives of employees unions.

(*c*) the employees should also try to be fair as regards some of the demands like, for example the demand for further increase of employees strength in the Corporation especially when 30,000 new employees have been appointed very recently in the Corporation inspite of the Corporation facing financial crunch already.

Opportunity for Growth, Innovation and Change

Every human being has the innate desire to have a shift from the routine and to do things differently, the work force in Corporation not being an exception. Opportunities provided for self growth help the workforce to keep themselves away from stagnation, change provides an opportunity for new learning and innovation helps to prove self worth. It has been found out that the opportunities made available to the workforce for their self and professional growth are limited in Tamil Nadu State Transport Corporation, Tirunelveli

District. The maximum opportunity made available for an employee is to become a shift supervisor and as per the statistics available, only two per cent of the entire population of drivers and conductors can become shift supervisors. It has been learnt that change of work is provided by shifting the routes given to the drivers and conductors frequently and by changing them from one shift to another. One has to strongly agree, after looking at the conditions prevailing in the Corporation, that the chances made available for employees to be innovative are practically nil as the employees are always struggling to meet the enhanced work standards prescribed for execution.

SUGGESTIONS

With a view to improve the prevailing condition it may be suggested that :

(*a*) the existing opportunity availability to climb the ladder for reaching the position of shift supervisor should be extended from two per cent to five per cent.

(*b*) the Management can invite suggestions from the employees to carry out the tasks differently, interestingly and profitably. Opportunities provided for this purpose will have a double edge in satisfying the egoistic needs of individual employees and the functional targets of the Corporation.

(*c*) the prevailing method of changing the employees from one shift to the other should be done after considering the request of individuals. This will help to promote understanding and cordiality among the stakeholders of the Corporation.

Social values and beliefs

The acceptance of personal and social values are important for the creation of an orderly society by which amity and prosperity can be promoted among its members. In the same way, the beliefs found among the members of the society can also influence their behaviour in the right direction, especially for the betterment of the individuals and the society. The level of social values and beliefs possessed by the work force in Tamil Nadu State Transport Corporation, Tirunelveli District is found to be satisfactory which is statistically supported in the findings under this dimension. The work force in the Corporation has concern regarding the increasing rate of road accidents involving buses and also for the family condition of the deceased in case of accidents. They are also for maintaining cordial relationship with the public in general and commuters in particular. They have expressed their view that the public should not be heavily charged through fare hikes just to compensate the loses of the Corporation. They also bring out their social bent of mind through organising awareness programmes for school going children on road safety, first aid etc. Their readiness and concern for the creation of an equalitarian society are proof of their possessing social values and beliefs.

Suggestions

The following are the suggestions to improve the social values and beliefs found among the work force of the Corporation:

(*a*) the Management and the employees' unions can jointly identify a few awareness programmes to be organised in the interest of the society.

(*b*) the work force can be encouraged to take an active part in organising such public programmes on first aid and road safety etc.

(*c*) the Management can institute awards e.g. 'Good citizenship award' for the employees with a view to enhance the social values and beliefs possessed already by the workforce.

Professional and Corporational Esprit

The prosperity of a civilised society is determined by many factors and one among them is the cordiality prevailing among its members. The employees in the Corporation should also promote be united among themselves and unity with the management. Such a situation would enable Corporation to enhance financial stability and happiness among its members and steady growth in its operations. The situation prevailing in the Corporation enables the researcher to understand that at present the Corporation's unity to be brought out jointly by the employees and the management of the Corporation is not satisfactory. There are initiatives on the part of the employees' unions to keep the work force united, so that they can reasonably bargain with the management. It is due to confrontations between the management and the employees over issues like fixation of responsibility for the poor show in operational efficiency, increasing expenditure, disagreement in workloads fixation etc., the unity between the Management and employees is deteriorating day by day.

SUGGESTIONS

It may be suggested in this regard that :

(*a*) both the management and the work force should realise that the destiny of the Corporation lies in their unity.

(*b*) the work force and the management should be ready to make compromises in their demands in the interest of the Corporation which sustains thousands of employees.

(*c*) the management and the employees' unions should jointly organise celebration occasions and conduct events which will help to promote understanding among them.

Management behaviour

The overall presentation of self before others through words and deeds decides the worth of a person and his acceptance in the society. In a work environment, the cordiality to be promoted between the employees and the management depends on how they enable others to project themselves and how they deal with one another in the process of interaction over different issues. It has been understood that the Management has enough reasons to justify their behaviour towards the work force, like continuous loss to the Corporation, increasing expenditure, mounting interest on borrowings and the unco-operative and lethargic attitude of the workforce, whereas the employees of the Corporation have a strong negative conviction over the way the management deals with issues like workload, fixation of responsibility for route collections, mounting pressure to cover extended kilometres per litre of diesel and decisions taken by the management concerning the work.

Suggestions

The following are the suggestions offered to improve the overall behaviour of the management and to develop a favourable perception towards the workforce:

(*a*) the management can think of having a round of discussions with the employees to explain the reasons behind certain developments and thereby can gain voluntary acceptance and willing co-operation from the workforce.

(*b*) instead of trying to find solutions for problems by blaming the employees and earning their displeasure, the management can find out the areas where they can improve.

(*c*) both the parties should understand that it is co-operation among them which is going to provide long life to the Corporation and thereby continuous means for the survival of the work force.

Events and Celebrations

It is no doubt that joyous occasions in life add strength to life and they promote a state of longing for such occasions to happen in our life again and again. Celebration of events and occasions produces pleasant feelings and promotes understanding and thereby it paves way for creating an atmosphere for prosperity and all round development. The study enables the researcher to understand that the employees of Tamil Nadu State Transport Corporation, Tirunelveli District have a positive attitude towards celebration of events and occasions in the premises of the Corporation but they lack co-operation from the side of the Management. Due to certain practical difficulties the management does not encourages such celebrations by and large, even though it permits whole heartedly the celebrations like '*Ayudha pooja*' within the premises of the Corporation. Against this back ground a majority of the workforce leave the depot to join their families, leaving only a small group of employees to celebrate the occasion within the premises of the Corporation. Most of the employees leave for home as soon as their duty is over and they spend a very little time in the Corporation premises along with their colleagues in sharing and caring among each other.

SUGGESTIONS

It may be suggested in this connection that

(*a*) the management should analyse the problems involved in organising events and celebrations in the premises of the Corporation and try to remove the practical difficulties associated with the same as it will enable creation of a conducive climate in the place of work.

(*b*) the unions of employees should also work along with the management to identify and overcome the difficulties involved in organising events and celebrations in the premises of the Corporation.

(*c*) the employees should also be made to realise that organising functions for events such as retirement, achievements etc., should promote unity among themselves, with the Management and thereby a pleasant climate for work in the Corporation.

Non-work related factors

The growth of an organisation depends on the prevailing internal environment which generally gets influenced by the work and non-work related factors. There is no doubt in the role of work related factors in influencing the quality of work climate in an organisation. On the other hand it has to be understood that the non-work related factors can also play a vital role in the determination of the nature and the quality of the job climate in an organisation. Aspects such as difference in treatment extended on the basis of caste, economical status, alcoholism, political interference, unethical behaviour of stake holders, religious affiliation and physical threats extended are generally considered as non-work related factors and the role of these factors in influencing the work climate in the Corporation is significant. The non-work related factors which should influence the climate in the Corporation have to be closely monitored and removed.

SUGGESTIONS

The following are the suggestions made by the researcher to improve the condition related to the non-work related factors:

(*a*) since a group of employees are under the debt traps of private money lenders who sometimes forcefully snatch the salary received by the employees at the gate, efforts should be taken both by the Management and employees' union to start a thrift society and relieve the employees from the clutches of private money lenders.

(*b*) alcoholism is also found to be a problem among the employees especially after the work is over. Programmes focusing self awareness and development, yoga and meditation have to be organised to relieve the work force from such adverse situations

(*c*) the management should ensure that its functioning is totally free from political interference especially in promoting employees as shift supervisors.

To Improve the Impact of Socio-economic Factors in Perception

It has been identified in the study that the perception of the employees has been influenced highly by the socio-economic factors associated with them. The employees differ in their perception of organisational climate based on age, marital status, number of dependents, work experience etc. While accepting the role of these factors in perception, it has to be borne in mind that one cannot absolutely control or change the perception of others because the ability to exercise control over them by an external force is limited. On the other hand, it is suggested in this regard that the management should view certain issues affecting organisational climate very seriously and take stock of the situation. If the issues and the concern expressed by the employees are genuine, the management should take initiatives to set things aright and thereby ensure a healthy organisational climate in the corporation. If the situation appears contrary, the management should start educating the employees over the issue. Of course the success of building a conducive climate in any place of work requires mutual faith and concern shown by each other and the overall desire to add life to the existence of the job that acts as a source of their survival.

To Improve the Influence of Organisational Climate on Motivation and Performance of Employees

Any negative influence of organisational climate on motivation and performance is considered destructive as it hampers the progress. Any organisation which is in the process of scaling better heights should find a positive role of climate in inducing the motivation and performance of employees. The corporation in the given context should find out the ways and means of triggering motivation and performance of employees through a positive climate. In order to improve the climate in the corporation, the management should setup a Joint Action Committee consisting of the representatives of the employer and employees to look into the issue seriously and remove the obstacles in the process of building a conducive organisational climate and thereby contributing considerably towards motivation and performance of employees.

To Improve the Employees Perception of the Dimensions of Organisational Climate and the Possession of Basic Job Requisites

Perception on people, process and events will not happen in a vacuum. It is a product of accumulation and interpretation of information in a given context. The strength and weakness that one has, will influence his perception towards information available on people and events. More particularly, the understanding of one's knowledge and capabilities in a job will influence his perception of the dimensions of organisational climate. Efforts should be taken by the management of the corporation to improve the knowledge and capabilities of employees. Initiatives such as arranging for exposure programmes such as work shops, conferences and training on the latest developments in the job will improve their understanding of the work and thereby an improved perception towards the various dimensions of organisational climate.

To Improve the Different Aspects of Work Life

The three major aspects ranked as affecting the prevailing organisational climate are 'Increased work load', 'Targeted route collection', and 'Coverage of targeted kilometres per litre of diesel'. The following suggestions are forwarded to the management of the corporation to overcome such problems and thereby improve the climate in the place of work:

1. Sufficient number of employees should be recruited for the different vacancies in the corporation.
2. Efforts should be taken to cut down the expenses arising out of improper planning of activities.

3. Employees should be motivated positively to improve the route collection
4. Sufficient monetary and non-monetary rewards be extended to get the willing co-operation of the employees.
5. The management of the corporation should improve the working condition of buses and take into account the condition of traffic and roads while fixing the coverage of targeted kilometers per litre of diesel.

CONCLUSION

The quality of life that people lead is not decided by the possession of wealth and exteriors but by the presence of an environment to make use of such wealth and exteriors to lead a happy and contented life. Corporation as a composite entity cannot grow and reach greater heights by the mere possession of its resources. In the present study an attempt has been made to find out the nature of work climate present in Tamil Nadu State Transport Corporation, Tirunelveli District and an analysis has also been made to find out the factors contributing towards the prevalence of the particular climate in the study area. It is on the basis of these factors the researcher has put forward suggestions for the improvement of the overall climate in the Corporation. The researcher is confident that the management of the Tamil Nadu State Transport Corporation, Tirunelveli District which represents the department of Transport, Tamil Nadu will consider the suggestions given to enrich further the state of climate in the Corporation.

Any study conducted covering one aspect throws light over other issues and the researcher has in the process of conducting this study, identified some other connected issues deserving an in-depth study. The following areas are suggested for undertaking similar studies in Tamil Nadu State Transport Corporation, Tirunelveli District.

1. Organisational climate and perceived stress level among employees.
2. Organisational climate and productivity.
3. Organisational climate and service quality.
4. Organisational climate and support for innovation.

Bibliography

Aarons, Gregory A. and Angelina C. Sawitzky, 2006. "Organisational Climate Partially Mediates the Effect of Culture on Work Attitudes and Staff Turnover in Mental Health Services", *Administration and Policy in Mental Health and Mental Health Services Research,* Vol. 33, No. 3.

Afolabi, Olukayode Ayooluwa, 2005. "Influence of Organisational Climate and Locus of Control on Job Satisfaction and Turnover Intentions", *IFE Psychological* Vol. 13, No. 2.

Asha, S. 2008. "Organisational Climate and Employee Health", *The ICFAI Journal of Organisational Behaviour,* Vol. 7, No. 1.

Ashkanasy, Neal M, Wilderom, Celeste P.M, and Peterson, Mark F. 2000: *Handbook of Organisational Culture & Climate,* California : Sage Publications, Inc.

Burton, Richard M., Jorgen Lauridsen and Borge Obel, 2004. "The Impact of Organisational Climate and Strategic Fit on Firm Performance", *Human Resource Management,* Vol. 43, No. 1.

Chandran, J.S. 1998. *Organisational Behaviour,* New Delhi : Vikas Publishing House Private Limited.

Clark, Maira, 2002. "The Relationship between Employees' Perceptions of Organisational Climate and Customer Retention Rates in a Major UK Retail Bank", *Journal of Strategic Marketing,* Vol. 10, No. 7.

D'Amato, Alessia and Fred R.H. Zijlstra, 2008. "Psychological Climate and Individual Factors as Antecedents of Work Outcomes", *European Journal of Work and Organisational Psychology* , Vol. 17, No. 1.

Davidson, Michael C.G., 2003. "Does Organisational Climate Add to Service Quality in Hotels?", *International Journal of Contemporary Hospitality Management,* Vol. 15, No. 4.

Dawson, Jeremy F., Vincente Gonzalez-Roma, Ann Davis and Michael A. West 2008. "Organisational Climate and Climate Strength in UK Hospitals", *European Journal of Work and Organisational Psychology,* Vol. 17, No. 1.

De Clercq, Dirk and Imanol Belausteguigoitia Rius, 2007. "Organisational Commitment in Mexican Small and Medium Sised Firms: The Role of Work Status, Organisational Climate and Entrepreneurial Orientation", *Journal of Small Business Management*, Vol. 45, No. 4.

Dondero, Grace Marie, 1997. "Organisational Climate and Teacher Autonomy; Implications for Educational Reform", *International Journal of Educational Management*, Vol. 11, No. 5.

Elci, Meral and Lutfihak Alpkan, 2009. "The Impact of Perceived Organisational Ethical Climate on Work Satisfaction", *Journal of Business Ethics* , Vol. 84.

Fey, Carl F. and Paul W. Beamish, 2002. "Organisational Climate Similarity and Performance; International Joint Ventures in Russia", *Organisation Studies*, Vol. 22, No. 5.

Gray, Roderic J., 2001. "Organisational Climate and Project Success", *International Journal of Project Management*, Vol. 19, No. 2.

Griffith, James, 2008. "A Compositional Analysis of the Organisational Climate-Performance Relation: Public Schools as Organisations", *Journal of Applied Social Psychology*, Vol. 36, No. 8.

Haakonsson, Dorthe Dojbak, Richard Burton, Borge Obel, M. and Jorgen Lauridsen, 2008. "How Failure to Align Organisational Climate and Leadership Style Affects Performance", *Management Decisions*, Vol. 46, No. 3.

Halpin, A.W. 1996. Theory and Research in Administration, New York : Macmillan.

Hoy, Wayne K., James Hoffman, Dennis Sabo and James Bliss, 1996. "The Organisational Climate of Middle Schools: The Development and Test of the OCDQ-RM", *Journal of Educational Administration*, Vol. 34, No. 1.

Hunt, Brian and Toni Ivergard, 2007. "Organisational Climate and Work Place Efficiency", *Public Management Review*, Vol. 9, No. 1.

Idogho, Philipa O. 2006. "Academic Staff Perception of the Organisational Climàte in Universities in Edo State, Nigeria", *Journal of Social Sciences*, Vol. 13, No. 1.

James, Lawrence R., Carol C. Choi, Chia-Huei Emily Ko, Patrick K. Mcneil, Matthew K. Minton, Mary Ann Wright And Kwang–II Kim, 2008. "Organisational and Psychological Climate: A Review of Theory and Research", *European Journal of Work and Organisational Psychology*, Vol. 17, No. 1.

Javier, Francisco Llorens Montes, Antonia Ruiz Moreno and Luis Miguel Molina Fernandez, 2004. "Accessing the Organisational Climate and

Contractual Relationship for Perceptions of Support for Innovation", *International Journal of Manpower*, Vol. 25, No. 2.

Kangis, Peter, Gordon, D. Williams, S. 2000. "Organisational Climate and Corporate Performance: An Empirical Investigation", *Management Decision* , Vol. 38, No. 8.

Kristin, Smith-Crowe, Michael J. Burke and Ronald S. Landis, 2003. "Organisational Climate as a Moderator of Safety Knowledge-Safety Performance Relationships", *Journal of Organisational Behaviour*, Vol. 24, No. 7.

Kunnanatt, James Thomas, 2007. "Impact of ISO 9000 on Organisational Climate : Strategic Change Management Experience of and Indian Organisation", *International Journal of Manpower*, Vol. 28, No. 2.

Litwin, G. and Stringer, R. 1968. *Motivation and Organisational Climate*, Boston : Harvard University Press.

Manorama, S, 1993. "Impact of Organisational Climate on Personnel Management in University Libraries", *Academic Libraries*, TR Publications Private Ltd, Chennai, 1993.

Nammi, A.Z. and Maryam Zarra Nezhad, 2009. "The Relationship between Psychological Climate and Organisational Commitment", *Journal of Applied Sciences*, Vol. 9, No. 1.

Neal, Andrew, Michael A. West and Malcolm G. Patterson, 2005. "Do Organisational Climate and Competitive Strategy Moderate the Relationship Between Human Resources Management and Productivity", *Journal of Management*, Vol. 31, No. 4.

Nwankwo, Sonny, Owusu-Frimpong, Nana, Ekwulugo and Frances, 2004. "The Effects of Organisational Climate on Market Orientation: Evidence from the Facilities Management Industry", *Journal of Service Marketing*, Vol. 18, No. 2.

Pashiardis, Georgia, 2008. "Toward a Knowledge Base for School Climate in Cyprus's Schools", *International Journal of Education Management*, Vol. 22, No. 5.

Patterson, Malcolm G., Michael A. West, Viv J. Shackleton, Jeremy F. Dawson, Rebecca Lawthom, Sally Maitlis, David L. Robinson and Alison M. Wallace, 2005. "Validating the Organisational Climate Measure: Links to Managerial Practices, Productivity and Innovation", *Journal of Organisational Behaviour*, Vol. 26, No. 4.

Patterson, Malcolm, Peter Warr and Michael West, 2004. "Organisational Climate and Company Productivity : The Role of Employee Affect and Employee Level", *Journal of Occupational and Organisational Psychology*, Vol. 77, No. 2.

Ross, Thomas, A. 1976. "The Organisational Climate of Schools", *International Review of Education*, Vol. 22, No. 4.

Schulte, Mathis, Ostroff, Cheri, Kinicki, Angelo, J. 2006. "Organisational Climate Systems and Psychological Climate Perceptions: A Cross-Level Study of Climate Satisfaction Relationships", *Journal of Occupation and Organisational Psychology*, Vol. 79, No. 4.

Shadur, Mark A., Rene Kienzle and John J. Redwell, 1999. "The Relationship between Organisational Climate and Employee Perceptions of Involvement", *Group and Organisation Management*, Vol. 24, No. 4.

Townsend, Barbara K., 2006. "Community College Organisational Climate for Minorities and Women", *Community College Journal of Research and Practice*, Vol. 30.

Uline, Cynthia and Megan Tschannen Moran, 2007. "The Walls Speak: The Interplay of Quality Facilities, School Climate and Student Achievement", *Journal of Educational Administration*, Vol. 46, No. 1.

Watkin, Chris and Ben Hubbard, 2003. "Leadership Motivation and the Drivers of Share Price : The Business Case for Measuring Organisational Climate", *Leadership and Organisation Development Journal*, Vol. 24, No. 7.

Yoon, Mahn Hee, Sharon E Beatty and Jaebeom Suh, 2001. "The Effect of Work Climate on Critical Employee and Customer Outcomes: An Employee Level Analysis", *International Journal of Service Industry Management*, Vol. 12, No. 5.

Index

R